FROM RAILWAY TO RUNWAY

Published in 2000 by
WOODFIELD PUBLISHING
Bognor Regis, West Sussex PO21 5EL, UK.

© Leslie Harris, 2000

ISBN 0 873203 60 8

From
Railway
to
Runway

Wartime diary of an RAF Observer

FLT/SGT LESLIE HARRIS

Woodfield Publishing
BOGNOR REGIS · WEST SUSSEX · ENGLAND

Introduction

I, Leslie David Harris, was born on 6th October 1943, three months after the death of my father, after whom I was named. My mother and grandmother hardly ever spoke to me about my father. When I was young I did not think anything of this, assuming that perhaps the subject was too painful for them.

It was not until a considerable time after my mother's death in 1976 that I discovered my father's letters and journals in a tin trunk in the loft of her house.

It came as a revelation to me to learn that the marriage of my mother and father took place in September 11th 1940 and of the birth of my elder brother Noel Anthony on 19th December 1940. With such a short time between these events I can only now understand why there was such a coolness between my mother and grandmother...

I have learned a lot about my father from his writings and now feel it is a great pity that those who knew him were unable or unwilling to tell me about him. As a consequence I do not know why my father and his mother moved to the Isle of Wight from Liverpool after the death of my grandfather. I can only assume that it was because my grandmother had relatives on the Island. I have vague childhood memories of the Auntie Rose and Uncle Bert mentioned in the writings.

Apparently, my father and mother met on the 29th of August 1939 in Shanklin. Vague memories make me think that my mother was doing some sort of shop work at the Co-op store in Shanklin and was staying with a Mr & Mrs Beddows in Shanklin at the time. I believe that I met them in my childhood days.

Leslie's mother (my grandmother) continued to live in Lake, Isle of Wight until the late 1950s. She married a second time to Frank Barton, a railwayman, and for a time ran the refreshment room at Ventnor station, of which I also have fond memories. They both moved to St. Margaret's, near Richmond, London, when the IOW Railway suffered in the 'Beeching cuts'. My (honorary) Uncle Frank then worked as a railwayman at Richmond, finally retiring and working as a gardener (he was also a trained Nurseryman) until his death in the mid 1960s. My grandmother returned to the Island and died there in 1968.

My mother, Monica, was left to bring up two small children almost single-handed and life was very hard for her in every respect. As a direct consequence, I believe, her health suffered. She died of emphysema at Rye Hospital in 1976, aged 67.

My elder brother, Noel, attended Queen Elizabeth Grammar School at Faversham in Kent and then took an Apprenticeship as a Paper Maker at the local Mill at Kemsley which, I believe, was owned by Bowaters at the time. Although qualifying, he discovered that promotion could only be achieved through filling the proverbial 'dead man's shoes'. Consequently, he left and joined a firm in the Midlands who imported French produce, with a view to training for a management position in due course. Unfortunately, part of his early duties entailed delivering produce by road. In 1967 the Transit van Noel was driving was in collision with a lorry. As a result, he was killed, at the age of just 27.

I attended Borden Grammar School in Sittingbourne and then joined the RAF as a Boy Entrant in 1960. I became a Clerk Secretarial, gained the rank of Corporal, but left the Air Force in 1973 at the expiration of my engagement, to allow me to look after my mother, whose health was by now, failing.

I commenced working for British Rail as a Clerical Officer and retired, on medical grounds, in 1994. Since then I have had the opportunity to study the writings left by my father and to prepare them for publication.

Les Harris, 2000

The diary of an Englishman in a time of war.
His story.
His beliefs.
His hopes.

By Leslie Harris, Esquire

At 'Saint Nicholas',
19, Louis Road,
Lake.
Isle of Wight
in the county of Hampshire.

The eleventh day of September in the year of our
lord, Nineteen Hundred, and Forty.

The frontispiece of Leslie's diary, written in his own handwriting.

Leslie Harris at No. 45 Air School, Oudtshoorn, South Africa, Sunday March 8th 1942. Mapping the route. "We do not wear full flying kit as it is too hot". (see page 179)

War – this is again wasting the world through the foolishness of mankind. Once more the shadow of death overcasts Europe and dims the eye of God. It is no way to settle disputes, for even if an army is defeated and a country destroyed, a tiny spark of freedom remains in every man of every race or creed, which by some gallant or misguided man will be fanned into a flame that will in its turn bring more fear and unhappiness.

The very people who should lead the way to unity which will bring peace to this blood-drenched earth – God's ministers – are divided among themselves, so who then can hold men's hearts but God alone.

If the Church is too weak and corrupt to be of service to mankind, it is up to a council of experts to stop these petty quarrels and to unite once more, the holy office into one. Christ did not make Protestants, Catholics, Baptists, Methodists and the rest, but Christians. He did not have an archbishop or a bishop or a pope as a father, for did he not say that all his teachers were equal? How then can we live at peace with the clergy striving against one another for promotion instead of working for the good of everyone? Which is more sincere, the pomp and show of a cathedral or a true man speaking loyally to his God as friend speaks to friend, openly and unafraid? Is a good ruler feared by his subjects? How then, can we fear him who is the best ruler of all?

Even if you disbelieve in God as I myself have often done, is there not something in every one of us which tells us what is right and what is wrong? Make yourself a god by doing that which the great God would do if he was living on the earth. Once it was written in a book which most of us have read at one time or another about a character called Mrs Do-As-You-Would-Be-Done-By. If people would only remember this, war would be impossible.

Leslie Harris, aged 19
Alverstone Station, April 25th 1940

Leslie and Monica at the seaside, 1940.

Wednesday September 11th 1940: Monica and myself were married this afternoon at the Parish Church of Shanklin at four. In the morning Monica came to Lake to get everything ready. She left a note to say that my new suit had not yet arrived. As it was too late to do anything, I had to go in my other suit. The car arrived early but Mother and myself were ready. Owing to a misunderstanding the car took us straight to pick up Monica at Shanklin instead of going first to the church and then on to fetch Monica. The driver, a lady by the way, told us this was to save petrol by only making one journey instead of two, Even as we knelt at the altar during the service the Air Raid Warning shrieked and we heard the sound of aircraft battling overhead. The funny thing was that the Rector was so deaf that he did not realise that an air raid had taken place until the ceremony was over when we left the church. Later we returned home for tea and so, after a jolly evening, ended this happy day.

Thursday September 12th 1940: This evening Mother told me the sad news that Sidney Pinkstone had been killed in a motor smash yesterday afternoon, I am very sorry, for he was a good friend of mine and often we had been out shooting rabbits.

Friday September 13th 1940: On guard duty at Sandown station from 10.30pm to 4.30am on Saturday. The air raid warning sounded before I left home, and there was much gun fire during the night.

Saturday September 14th 1940: Beginning to get settled into married life. Monica is a very good cook and everything else.

Sunday September 15th 1940: Dug up the rest of the potatoes this morning. Otherwise have had a quiet day.

Monday September 16th 1940: The funeral of young Pinkstone took place today. Mrs Pinkstone came into Alverstone station in the afternoon and I offered my condolences.

Tuesday September 17th 1940: I was up a little late so have done nothing before going off to work after lunch.

Wednesday September 18th 1940: Picked quite a lot of blackberries for Mother and Monica from the bushes around the station.

Thursday September 19th 1940: Bicycled to Sandown this morning to change my book at the library.

Friday September 20th 1940: Went again into Sandown after breakfast. Called at the newsagents for my four weekly books, but only two were there, as yet.

Saturday September 21st 1940: The 8.10 train was very late today, it was nearly 8.30 before it departed from Alverstone.

Sunday September 22nd 1940: Mother went to visit Aunt Rose in the afternoon. Later in the evening the air raid warning sounded and the anti-aircraft guns went into action. I rode into Shanklin to find out if Mother and Aunt Rose were safe. They were, and Mother decided to stay overnight to keep Aunt Rose company. I had to go on Local Defence Volunteer duty at 10.30pm so Monica was alone until I came back at about 4.30am on Monday morning.

Monday September 23rd 1940: Played "conkers" with the children at the station in the evening. I also caught a toad, but I let it go again.

Tuesday September 24th 1940: During the morning German aircraft made a large scale raid against Southampton. From Alverstone station I saw five hostile aircraft , under heavy AA fire, travelling towards Southampton. Later I saw aircraft returning but they were too far away to be identified. At the newsagents one of my books, due last Friday, arrived this afternoon, but the Radio Times is not in yet.

Wednesday September 25th 1940: Mother went to Shanklin again today and stayed the night there. I spent the afternoon cataloguing my stamp collection.

Thursday September 26th 1940: When I got to the station, I telephoned Mother to make sure that she was alright.

Friday September 27th 1940: Went shopping in Sandown this afternoon with Monica.

Saturday September 28th 1940: I left the station a little earlier so as to be able to go over to Ashey with Mr Fowler and two other members of the LDV, for bayonet drill.

Sunday September 29th 1940: My Sunday off duty today, but we have not been out all day.

Monday September 30th 1940: Went into Sandown this morning to fetch the rest of my weekly books from the newsagents.

Tuesday October 1st 1940: On L.D.V. duty again today. During the night there was quite a lot of gunfire towards Portsmouth and Southsea.

Wednesday October 2nd 1940: Took Monica to the Rivoli cinema in Shanklin this evening to see "The Return of the Invisible Man". It was excellent.

Thursday October 3rd 1940: The gang came down to the station this evening and bought some potatoes with them. We roasted these on the fire for supper. After the last train had left I went home to another supper.

Friday October 4th 1940: The boys were down to see me at the station this evening.

Saturday October 5th 1940: The day, but one, to my holidays. I am looking forward to them.

Sunday October 6th 1940: It has been a very wet day today. During the afternoon I have been at the station and in the evening Monica, Mother and I played cards.

Monday October 7th 1940: Went over to Southampton on the 11am and came back at about 7pm. There was much damage done in Southampton and Woolston. I saw whole streets of houses knocked over and burnt. The greatest loss I saw was a Supermarine aircraft factory destroyed, with the burnt remains of several aeroplanes still inside. On the way back I saw the French battleship "Paris" in Portsmouth harbour. Just as I got off the train at Sandown I heard an aircraft approaching and then the air raid warning sounded followed shortly by the explosion of three bombs from the direction of Borthwood.

Tuesday October 8th 1940: This morning I went out to Borthwood to examine the damage done last night. A stable was destroyed and a horse was killed. A roof was taken off a house and dozens of windows were broken. I managed to obtain part of one of the bombs.

Wednesday October 9th 1940: This morning I rode to Sandown and brought one or two stamps which I later mounted in my albums.

Thursday October 10th 1940: Went with Monica to the Queens cinema tonight to see a film called "Bulldog". It was very good.

Friday October 11th 1940: In the afternoon Monica and myself went out to Borthwood Coppice to gather nuts. We got quite a lot. On LDV duty at 10.30 tonight with Mr Mantel. Mr Fowler had a uniform for me, but it was much too small. He also gave me a field dressing in case it is ever needed.

Saturday October 12th 1940: Went this afternoon on the 3.6pm train from Sandown to Horringford. There we took part in field exercises and hand grenade throwing. We returned by the 5.28pm train. As Mr Mantel was going on to Newport I gate him one and ninepence to get my badges for me. Mr Fowler gave me the other two cloth badges, so all I want now is a uniform.

Sunday October 13th 1940: In the afternoon I fixed a towel rack in the bathroom for Mother.

Monday October 14th 1940: I found that Mr Mantel had put the badges through the letter box before we were up this morning. Went back to work this afternoon but as there was very little to do. I went boating with the children after the 6.11 train had left.

Tuesday October 15th 1940: The boys went to the films tonight so I have been alone at the station.

Wednesday October 16th 1940: Took Monica to see the film "Crimes at the Dark House" at the Queens this evening. I enjoyed it very much. It was raining hard when we left home so we went by bus to Sandown.

Thursday October 17th 1940: At 10.30 this morning, when Monica and myself were having breakfast, we heard aircraft passing overhead. Almost at once we heard the whistling noise of three bombs hurtling down, We took cover on the floor and felt the concussion of only two detonations. We then went upstairs and found that some plaster had been shaken from the ceiling of Mother's room.

Looking out of the window we saw smoke rising from the direction of Sandown Railway Station. I hurried off in case this had been hit but, luckily, they had landed in an open field. Two of them were HE (High Explosive) and the other was an oil bomb which had failed to catch light. This accounted for the fact that we only heard two explosions.

Friday October 18th 1940: It rained very hard this evening so Jack and Marcus offered to go up the line to extinguish the signal lamp as the 8.11pm passed. Unfortunately the train was over twenty minutes late so they were soaked by the time they got back to the station.

Saturday October 19th 1940: I went along to see the hole made by the bomb which fell on Lake Green on Thursday. It is much larger than those I saw on Thursday. I was on LDV duty tonight with Mr Mantel. We took the first turn from 10.30pm to 2.15am then two other volunteers took over until 6am.

Sunday October 20th 1940: On getting here about 6.30am I told Monica that I was going out again to get a few mushrooms for breakfast. I spent quite a time out in the fields but I only found a few. I was on duty this afternoon at the station and after tea we played darts.

Monday October 21st 1940: Monica gave me breakfast in bed this morning and we spent a pleasant afternoon together. A churn of milk belonging to Ron Barton was found to be sour and it was returned on the 4.57pm train. After the 6.11pm train had passed Merstone I walked, with Jack, to Kern Farm to inform Ron about it.

Tuesday October 22nd 1940: Looked in at the station to see if my uniform had arrived but it had not. Mr Fowler suggested that I went into Newport to see about it.

Wednesday October 23rd 1940: Went on the 3.06pm train to Newport and saw Mr Harding. From him I obtained my LDV uniform, haversacks leggings, belt and blanket. I found a note in one of the pockets from a girl in Belfast, asking the finder to write to her, but of course I will not. In the evening Monica sewed the badges onto the jacket for me.

Thursday October 24th 1940: Went in my uniform, with Jack and Bill, to a Home Guard show in Newchurch. It was so dull I left long before it was over. While I was there I asked Bernice and Jack to come to tea on Sunday.

Friday October 25th 1940: Went shopping with Monica in Sandown this afternoon. I bought some stamps so have spent the evening with my albums.

Saturday October 26th 1940: Went to Newchurch by the 3.06pm train and took part in the LDV training there. Came back on the 5.34pm. Bombs were dropped on Ventnor and three also landed near to Perreton Farm.

Sunday October 27th 1940: Bernice and Jack arrived just after five and during an air raid alarm. After tea we played darts and cards until it was time for them to depart. Just before they left we heard eight explosions from the direction of Newport. On LDV duty from 10.30pm to 4.30am during which time bombs were heard bursting in Portsmouth.

Monday October 28th 1940: We could not get Newport station on the telephone although we tried several times during the night. In the morning we found out that the line was damaged and out of order. At 2.30am Boyce came down and we learnt from him that bombs had fallen at Newchurch. When I went on duty at 1.30pm I found buses running in place of trains, but the 3.51 ran as usual.

Tuesday October 29th 1940: Rode into Newchurch this morning to see the bomb damage. The two which fell nearest to the railway line were between Newchurch's Down Distant signal and Alverstone's Up Distant signal. A bomb had come down on each side of the rails but as the ground is nothing but marsh, the main explosion had only excavated large holes there. Pieces of the bombs had cut the rails and this was what had stopped the trains yesterday. More High Explosive bombs together with two oil bombs had been dropped towards Kniton.

Wednesday October 30th 1940: Eileen got married to Jim in Shanklin this afternoon. We missed Jack and Bernice at the station so we went to the Rivoli where we saw a film called "Counterfeit". It was only fairish.

Thursday October 31st 1940: Very quiet today.

Friday November 1st 1940: There was a great air battle overhead early this afternoon and two aircraft were seen to fall. I went over to see the mill kittens and picked one for myself. Delivered some goods to Hill Cottage and on the way back as it was getting dark I got lost in the bog. Luckily I got back in time for the 7.34pm train. Bombs were heard to fall on Shanklin just before eight. On the way home it rained hard so I got very wet.

Saturday November 2nd 1940: Went into Sandown this morning to fetch my books. While I was there I changed Mother's library book for her. Mother told me that the bombs had hit the Napier hotel and that one had fallen in St Saviours grounds. There were no casualties.

Sunday November 3rd 1940: I have been at the station today so have not done anything but knock about the house.

Monday November 4th 1940: On LDV duty from 10.30pm to 4.30am this morning. A quiet night, so nothing to report.

*November 1940: Leslie dressed for LDV (Home Guard) duty
outside 'St Nicholas', Lake, Isle of Wight.*

Tuesday November 5th 1940: Very quiet day. Not even an air raid to liven up Guy Fawkes day.

Wednesday November 6th 1940: There was a large air battle here during the afternoon. I saw one of our planes come down in flames. I cycled out to find it and found it blazing in a field not far from Horringford station. The pilot was dead and the aircraft a total loss. On the way back my cycle got a puncture in the rear tyre, so Uncle Bert gave me a lift to Sandown in the Goods train.

Thursday November 7th 1910: Monica's sister Nora arrived just after lunch and during an air raid. A number of aircraft were engaged overhead and one of our planes was brought down in the sea off Green Tiles. The pilot was unhurt. I went along to see it and only the tail was sticking out of the water. Another RAF plane came down near Pereton Farm.

Friday November 8th 1940: Got up early this morning and went by the 6.55am train from Sandown. I arrived at Waterloo at about 10.30am, All the glass in the roof of the station has been blown out and the walls outside are pitted with holes from bursting bombs. I went by bus over Westminster bridge and looked at the Houses of Parliament. A bomb crater was not very far from Big Ben. I walked up Whitehall and past Nelson's column where there were two more craters in the road. I had lunch at an ABC café before going on up Fleet Street. I went in St. Paul's Cathedral and saw the damage made by the bomb which hit the roof. Next I went down into the crypt and saw the tombs of many great people. I called to see the Bank of England which was also hit by bombs. From here I went by tube train to the Elephant and Castle and after getting on the wrong one I got out and walked to the Imperial War Museum. This had also been hit by bombs so I could not go inside. Next I went by bus to Baker Street to see Madame Tussauds but once again, this was closed

Friday November 8th 1940

...t up early this morning, and went by the 6.55 P.M. train from
...ndown. I arrived at Waterloo about half passed ten. All
...e glass in the roof of the station has been blown out, and
...e walls outside are pitted with holes from bursting bombs.
...I went by 'bus over Westminster Bridge, and looked at the
...uses of Parliment. A bomb crater was not very far from Big
...n. I walked up Whitehall, and past Nelson's column where
...ere were two more craters in the road.
...Then I had lunch at an A.B.C. shop before going on up
...et Street.
...I went in 'St Paul's', and saw the damage made by the bomb
...ich hit the roof. Next I went down into the crypt and
...w the tombs of many great people.
...I called to see "The Bank of England" which also was hit
...y bombs. From here I went by tube train to "Elephant and
...stle", and after getting on the wrong one I managed to
...t out, and walk to "The Imperial War Museum". This had
...lso been hit by bombs so I could not go inside.
...Next I went by 'bus to Baker Street to see "Madame
...ssauds", but once again this was closed owing to bomb damage.
...Then as I was getting fed up I took the 'bus back to Waterloo
...d came home on the 4.45 P.M.

Saturday November 9th 1940

...d one or two odd jobs about the house before into Sandown
...get my books.
...Again after dinner I rode into the town this time to buy
...few foreign stamps for my collection.

owing to bomb damage. Then, as I was getting fed up, I took the bus back to Waterloo and came home on the 4.45pm train.

Saturday November 9th 1940: Did one or two odd jobs about the house before going into Sandown to get my books. After dinner I rode into the town., this time to buy a few foreign stamps for my collection.

Sunday November 10th 1940: It has been too wet to go out so have spent the morning clearing the cupboard under the stairs. In the afternoon I sorted out the stamps I got yesterday.

Monday November 11th 1940: Spent this morning tidying up the garden shed and then went back on duty at the station at 1.30pm.

Tuesday November 12th 1940: After supper tonight I went on LDV duty until 4.30am. A quiet night, but three Policemen came down to our guard room for a cup of tea as it was very cold outside.

Wednesday November 13th 1940: As soon as I got home this morning I went up to bed and, as I was on late duty, nothing else is worth writing about.

Thursday November 14th 1940: When I arrived at the station at 5.30 this morning I found the rail track under water and the house flooded. Walked a little way down the track in Wellington boots and rescued a field mouse from drowning, When I went home I took it with me and let it free in the garden. No trains ran all day. In the evening Monica and myself went to see a film called "Elizabeth and Essex" at the Queen's cinema. It was very good.

Friday November 15th 1940: By the tune I got to the station this afternoon the flood had receded but Squibb told me that the first train was the 11.18am. Of course buses ran both yesterday and today in place of the cancelled trains.

Saturday November 16th 1940: Normal train service, but the water is still over the river banks and it rained hard at times.

Sunday November 17th 1940: Flood again today but not so bad as before. No trains, so a bus ran again. It brought me home at 5.30pm so I got home earlier than usual.

Monday November 18th 1940: The water stopped the trains until the 11.18am. Bombs fell at Gurnard with at least 18 casualties. Damage was done to the cement mills near Newport. Others hit the railway line near Whippingham and stopped traffic to Ryde. The Goods train had to come round Alverstone way. Also a dud anti-aircraft shell landed in Sharp' s Timber Yard at Sandown. I left my shoes behind when I went off this morning to work in my Wellington boots. Monica kindly took my shoes to Sandown station and they sent them down on the 12.11pm train, Went for a walk this afternoon with Monica to Shanklin. While we were there we bought some fish off some fishermen on the foreshore. Then we went to see the Napier hotel which had been hit by the bombs dropped on November 1st.

Tuesday November 19th 1940: Bombs were reported to have been dropped near to St. Lawrence tunnel. Did a little gardening before tea and then went on LDV duty from 10.30 to 4.30am.

Wednesday November 20th 1940: As soon as I came off guard duty I had breakfast and went off to work. The weather was not too good today as it rained most of the time.

Thursday November 21st 1940: Late turn today so I did not get up very early. It has rained for most of the day again.

Photo courtesy of the Isle of Wight Steam Railway Collection.

Photo courtesy of the Isle of Wight Steam Railway Collection.

Alverstone station on the Isle of Wight Railway in the 1930s (above) and below Leslie poses with a colleague near the station.

Friday November 22nd 1940: Got a kitten from the Mill at Alverstone today. I brought it home and have called it Figgaro. In the afternoon went shopping in Sandown with Monica. While I was there I changed Mother's book at the library for her. There was an LDV meeting from 7pm to 9pm which I attended. Mr Fowler asked me if I would represent the Section at a Company competition. I agreed at once. Just before the meeting began, we saw a German plane caught in the beams of a number of searchlights, but it soon got away.

Saturday November 23rd 1940: There was a very heavy frost this morning and, for the first time this season, saw ice about.

Sunday November 24th 1940: Spent today indoors reading and in the evening playing cards with Monica.

Monday November 25th 1940: Very little doing today. It has been very cold and frosty.

Tuesday November 26th 1940: Mr Smith gave me some turnips which I sent to Sandown by train. I went to see Mr Fowler and got permission from him to bring one of the Lee Enfield .303 rifles home when I come off duty tomorrow.

Wednesday November 27th 1940: Early turn of duty at the station today. There was to have been a lecture about machine guns at Sandown station, but it was cancelled. On LDV duty again this night. It was exceedingly cold during the night. Brought a rifle, number 402619, home, as arranged yesterday.

Thursday November 28th 1940: The Germans made an air attack on Portsmouth during the afternoon. Their aircraft were intercepted over the Island by British planes and a battle of some size ensued. Just before five, one of the German planes came out of the clouds with its port engine on fire. It was followed by a British fighting aircraft pumping lead into it as it went down. It crashed in the sea off Ventnor.

Friday November 29th 1940: German aircraft were seen during the afternoon and under anti-aircraft fire, but no results are known. Bought a sack of potatoes for ten shillings from Mr Plumbley and sent them on the 3.51 train to Sandown.

Saturday November 30th 1940: Very heavy air attack on Southampton. Great damage and loss of life.

Sunday December 1st 1940: Air attack resumed as soon as dark fell. Again against Southampton. Meant to make a note yesterday that I fetched the potatoes from Sandown station. Spent the evening playing cards.

Monday December 2nd 1940: I went this evening to a lecture, held at the LDV Headquarters, on the Browning automatic rifle. My cold is no better so went to bed as soon as I got back again.

Tuesday December 3rd 1940: Went to the Rivoli with Mother to see the film "The Last Train from Munich". It was very good indeed. Mr Times, my old schoolmaster, and his daughter, sat just in front of us. Air raid from just before six until about 8.20pm. My cold made me feel not too well, so I went to bed as soon as I got home.

Wednesday December 4th 1940: Fifteen to twenty incendiary bombs were dropped on Alverstone at about 7.15 last night. They landed in the Lynch and surrounding fields. As it was raining at the time the undergrowth was wet so did not take fire. No damage. After the 7.45am train I cycled up to the Lynch and found parts of the fins of one of the bombs. LDV duty from 10.30 to 4.30am tonight. It was very quiet.

Thursday December 5th 1940: Changed over turns of duty with Squibb today so that I could go to bed as soon as I got home this morning. That is why I was at Alverstone when hostile aircraft dropped two bombs on it. I was in the office at about seven when I heard the now familiar sound of falling missiles. I dropped under the table and was shaken by the ensuing explosions. Rushing out I saw a pillar of fire blazing towards Alverstone Farm. Jumping on my cycle up I went to see about it. The oil bomb which was burning in the road by Plumbley's Barn had demolished a wall and damaged Price's house. Mr Plumbley, Mr Halsey and myself put out the fire by shovelling earth on it. I threw bricks from the wall down into the crater. We had it out long before anyone else arrived. We knew that an HE bomb had exploded nearby but we were unable to locate it. This I reported to the Signalman at Merstone. He held the 7.34pm train until I walked along the railway line to the water works to ascertain that the way was clear. By the time the 8.11 train came back it was after 9pm. I brought a large piece of the oil bomb home. On arriving home Monica told me that Mr Barwell had delivered our fruit bushes.

Friday December 6th 1940: The HE bomb crater was found this morning between Plumbley's house and Alverstone Farm. We were all amazed at the immense size of the hole. Estimates varied from 15 feet deep and 30 feet wide to 30 feet by 50 feet. I myself judged it to be about 20 feet by 45 feet. At home Monica and myself decided to plant the fruit bushes but, before we had a chance, it began to rain.

Saturday December 7th 1940: I went to Ryde this afternoon to see an exhibition of weapons of war in the Town Hall. I saw and examined the following: the Browning gun, the Lewis gun, the Bren gun, the Thompson sub-machine gun, the anti-tank rifle and two types of mortars. Altogether I enjoyed it. Afterwards I walked down to St. John's Road station, buying a pot of marmalade for Monica on the way. I saw the damage done by Thursday's raid. One or two houses were down and hundreds of windows were broken.

Sunday December 8th 1940: Not much doing today, Mother went to Shanklin yesterday evening and will not be back until tomorrow morning. I had a bath before breakfast but nothing else has happened as yet to write about.

Monday December 9th 1940: Planted the seven fruit bushes in the garden this morning, then I rode into Sandown and changed both Mother's and my own books at the library.

Tuesday December 10th 1940: During the afternoon saw a German plane under AA fire flying away from Portsmouth towards the South. It escaped safely. Three of our aircraft came up afterwards but they were much too late, and so they returned after a short while. On LDV duty from 10.30pm to 4.30am tonight.

Wednesday December 11th 1940: At the station this morning we had the Waiting Room as a guard room. It was much better than the Porter's room. First air raid for some days this evening. On my way home from the station, about nine, I heard aircraft passing overhead, followed by bombs dropped towards Brading.

Letter to Los Angeles, California, USA:

Dear Auntie Ciss,

This letter is long overdue but I hope you will forgive us as these times are very hectic. We hope you are all in the best of health. Mother has a cold, but, beyond that, we are quite fit, I expect you have read in your newspapers all about the German raids on our cities and towns, Well I have been to London and Southampton as well as to

Portsmouth in the last few days. A great deal of damage has been done and the loss of life is very heavy, but we only curse the Germans and fight on.

Last Thursday incendiary bombs were dropped around the railway station where I work. Some fell in a wood and two trees took fire, but this was soon put out. It was raining at the time so the undergrowth was too wet to burn and the bombs soon burnt out, Not satisfied with this, two nights later the foe bombed the locality again. I should have said that the station is only a small one and only one of us is on duty at a time. It was just after seven when I was alone in the office I heard the drone of hostile aircraft followed by the now familiar sound of falling missiles. I dropped under a table and was shaken by the ensuing explosion. The windows blew out and I was covered by glass but, luckily, I was not cut at all. Rushing outside I saw a pillar of fire blazing towards a farm not 50 yards away.

Up I ran to see about it and found it was an oil bomb which was burning in the roadway. Two other fellows came up and, between us, we put out the fire by shovelling earth onto it. The bomb had demolished a wall and damaged the farm buildings, but, thank God, no one was hurt. My hands were burnt and my hair singed, but that was all.

An HE bomb had also fallen, but it landed in a field and did no harm. When the bomb crater was measured in the morning it was found to be 50 feet across by 30 feet deep. The Germans are overhead again tonight. I wonder where they are going now?

Well, I must close now by wishing you the best of all for Xmas.

The above letter was returned to sender a few days later.

It had been Censored by Examiner 5838 who enclosed a form PC105 which read:

> *"It is important that information should not be allowed to pass out of Great Britain as to the exact locality in which damage has been done by enemy air raids, and it is even more important that no information should pass as to the date or time at which damage was done at a particular place. Any such information is likely to be of great value to the enemy if it should come to his knowledge. You are therefore requested to abstain from making any mention of air raid damage in your correspondence."*

Thursday December 12th 1940: I was on early turn of duty at Alverstone today. About 10am a German observation plane flew over on a reconnaissance to view the damage they did at Portsmouth last night. The AA guns put up a very heavy barrage, but it passed through safely and returned to its base. When Squibb arrived he told me the bombs last night were two Delayed Action bombs which landed near to the main road so no traffic is allowed that way into Ryde, or from there to Sandown.

Friday December 13th 1940: Went into Sandown this morning to fetch my books and order two hundredweight of coal. While I was there I tried to buy a map of the Island, but no one had one. Squibb told me that the two DA bombs were safely removed from Brading yesterday afternoon.

Saturday December 14th 1940: Monica got me a mapping pen, ink, and a sheet of paper so I have started to draw myself a map. Quiet at the station as the boys went off to Sandown tonight.

Sunday December 15th 1940: What with getting up late and being on duty this afternoon, I have nothing to write about.

Monday December 16th 1940: Up at four this morning to get to the station by 5.30am. Nothing else to report.

Tuesday December 17th 1940: I went shopping with Monica and ordered a stamp catalogue from Broumonts this afternoon. In the evening I went to an LDV talk in Sandown with Mr Fowler and a few of the others.

Wednesday December 18th 1940: Spent a quiet afternoon by writing and mounting a few stamps. Just before we went to bed Monica said she felt queer, and would not be surprised if the baby was born tonight.

Thursday December 19th 1940: Luckily I was late turn today for I had to get up about three in the morning and go out in the rain to 'phone for the nurse. It was a false alarm for the baby arrived at 4.30 in the afternoon. Monica is quite alright after it all. Air raid at about 9.30pm.

Friday December 20th 1940: Baby is doing fine and Nora (Monica's sister) is staying until tomorrow.

Saturday December 21st 1940: Nora left on the 8.55 train this morning while I was on duty. As Mother and myself sat up in Monica's bedroom all three of us heard bombs fall towards Sandown. When I went outside I could see nothing.

Sunday December 22nd 1940: As Monica cannot get up yet Mother did not go to Eileen's, but kindly did the cooking and housework. An English bomber crashed on Brading Down early this morning. Two out of the crew of three were killed. The other, the pilot, escaped by parachute and only suffered a broken ankle.

Proud father Leslie with baby Noel, pictured at the rear of 'St Nicholas, Lake, Isle of Wight, soon after Noel's birth on 19th December 1940.

Monday December 23rd 1940: Just before three this afternoon a German Dornier bomber flew over Alverstone so low I could easily see its black crosses. During the morning I rode into Sandown to see the damage done last Saturday. The roofs of one or two houses were partly blown off and a great many windows were broken but that was all worth noting.

Tuesday December 24th 1940: It has been freezing lately and next doors overflow pipe has been leaking and, it is now frozen into icicles. Went up on the Downs to see the remains of the plane this morning, It is so much broken up that it is hard to tell that it is an aeroplane.

Wednesday December 25th 1940: Christmas Day and, luckily, I have got this day free from duty. Of course, Monica is not up yet but Mother and myself spent most of the day up in the bedroom with her. Chicken and Xmas pudding for dinner and iced cake for tea. Afterwards we pulled the crackers and set off the indoor fireworks. I put a paper hat on Figgaro the kitten, but he soon pulled it off, and then went to sleep on the pieces. In the evening we listened to the radio and ate nuts, fruit and sweetmeats until it was time for bed. Monica and myself gave Mother a nightdress and a bed jacket, a handbag and a bowl. Monica is giving me a stamp catalogue but it is not yet at the shop. From Mother I received a pair of pyjamas.

Thursday December 26th 1940: A number of Xmas cards arrived for us. One was from Arthur who is in Gibraltar, Mother is not going back to the shop until Saturday so she kindly did the cooking today.

Friday December 27th 1940: Much the same as yesterday. Baby is doing fine.

Saturday December 28th 1940: The stamp catalogue arrived for me this morning. The letter that I wrote to Auntie Ciss in the USA was returned to me by the Censor because I mentioned the damage done at Alverstone on the 5th of this month.

Sunday December 29th 1940: My turn of duty at Alverstone today, but as the boys came down the time soon passed.

Monday December 30th 1940: Mother got up at four to see me off to work this morning for Monica is not quite fit as yet. I saw to lunch when I returned home about 2pm. In the evening I attended LDV drill at the station from seven until nearly nine. On the way home passed an army lorry towing a searchlight. It had stopped in the middle of the road at the foot of Lake Hill due to the engine breaking down. It was gone by the time I returned.

Tuesday December 31st 1940: It has now been reported that on Sunday night the German Air Force made a very large raid on London. Many buildings were set on fire and destroyed.

The year past – 1940: At the ending of the old year I pause to thank it for the joy it has given me even during the bleak days of war.

The future – 1941: So begins the new year. What does it hold for my dear ones and myself? May God grant that we all shall see the end of this war.

Wednesday January 1st 1941: Hogmanay is past, so three cheers for the new year. Thank heavens Monica is up and about again, also that baby is doing well.

Thursday January 2nd 1941: As I changed over duty with Squibb this morning we did not get up very early. The German war planes were over as soon as darkness fell and the AA guns put up the usual barrage. I saw a new idea of grouping the searchlights in twos or threes for the first time. That is probably why the lorry was towing a searchlight on Monday when it broke down.

Friday January 3rd 1941: Young Dan gave me a piece of AA shell this morning for my collection. In the afternoon I went shopping for Monica.

Saturday January 4th 1941: As I was cycling to Alverstone, at about five this morning, the guns were still in action against the Germans. The "raiders passed" signal went just before seven.

Sunday January 5th 1941: It has been very cold again during the night so we did not get up very early. Yesterday Nora sent me a bag full of stamps. They were mostly one penny and half penny stamps of King Edward from 1902 to 1904. It was very kind of her and I spent most of today sorting them out. One or two were quite nice and. among them was a 10 cent Green USA, valued at 12 shillings and sixpence.

Monday January 6th 1941: About 7.45pm, as I was walking with William up to the signal to put the lamp out, snow began to fall and by the time I left to go home, the snow was about one inch deep.

Tuesday January 7th 1941: As it is freezing, the snow has not melted so the blessed children were able to snowball me as they got off the train! I managed to hit one or two of them with my return fire. The road was so slippery that I came off my cycle by the waterworks.

Wednesday January 8th 1941: Got up at four this morning and was sick. It must have been the roast potatoes I ate yesterday at the station. They did taste a bit funny at the time. I soon got over it and went off to take first turn of duty at Alverstone. I went to sleep most of the afternoon. At seven I went to Sandown station for more drill. Before I left Mr Fowler gave me 25 rounds of .303 ball cartridges. Twenty were Winchester USA 174 grain Full Patch while the others were British Lee Enfield cartridges.

Thursday January 9th 1941: German aircraft were about early in the evening but, as a whole, it was a quiet night.

Friday January 10th 1941: A little before seven the Germans commenced to bomb the city of Portsmouth, which I witnessed from Alverstone station, as I was on duty at the time, They began by dropping flares which our gunners tried to shoot out, but failed. This was quickly followed by the reports of exploding HE bombs. The bombardment lasted until after eight. A few of our night fighters engaged the foe during the battle for I saw their tracer bullets flaming in the sky. Later in the night, a second wave attacked and it was the largest bombardment I have yet heard.

Saturday January 11th 1941: Reports concerning the damage done at Portsmouth during the night are beginning. The following came from reliable sources: (1) The Guild Hall was hit and what little remains standing is unsafe. (2) Gas, water and electricity are cut off. The Gasworks are said to be destroyed. (3) The Harbour station was hit and an electric train of two coaches fell through the pier down onto the mud. No one was in it at the time as the passengers had taken cover.

Sunday January 12th 1941: My turn to be on duty at Alverstone this afternoon. Was told by Newport Office that boats to Portsmouth from Ryde would only cross during daylight. This I believe is due to two small vessels having been sunk in the fairway.

Monday January 13th 1941: They have been dynamiting dangerous buildings over on the mainland, for we could hear the reports on the Island. After tea I went to drill at Sandown station from 7pm until 8.30pm.

Tuesday January 14th 1941: It is Monica's birthday, so I wish her health and happiness for ever. Mother and myself each gave her a pair of stockings. In the evening Mother kindly looked after Baby so we could go the Queens. The film was called "The Great Dictator". It was a farce against Germany and was very good indeed.

Wednesday January 15th 1941: As Baby is not gaining weight very much Nurse has put him on baby food for a time. Snow fell during the afternoon.

Thursday January 16th 1941: Changed over turns of duty with Squibb today so have been on late turn. I had to go slowly on my cycle for the roads were very slippery.

Friday January 17th 1941: Bombs were dropped at Blackwater about 11.45pm last night. They did no damage but blew all the books etc. from the shelves of the railway station there. In the afternoon Mrs Avery came in and looked after Baby while we went into Sandown. Monica ordered a perambulator to be sent here while I got my weekly books. Then, before we returned here, Monica called in at Mr Young's to register Baby. We are calling him Noel Anthony.

Saturday January 18th 1941: Bombs at Newchurch again last night or rather 2.30am this morning. They fell in a field and did no damage other than cutting the telephone wires. The Railway Ganger walked from Horringford about 6.30am to see if the line was safe. It was, so the freight train came through. It started to rain and this, on top of the snow, made the roads like glass.

Sunday January 19th 1941: Monica and myself took Baby out in his perambulator this afternoon. We went along the cliff path into Shanklin and returned the road way. As the weather was quite fine I enjoyed it very much.

Monday January 20th 1941: After being dry yesterday it made up for it by raining for most of the day. By the time I arrived at Alverstone the river was over its banks but not yet up to the railway line.

Tuesday January 21st 1941: Still raining and water slowly rising around the station at Alverstone. Have decided to join the RAF as a member of an aircrew, if I can.

Wednesday January 22nd 1941: The flood at Alverstone has now receded, so that's settled. As I have been on early turn today we walked into Shanklin to get Baby's Ration Book. On the way home we met Mother and Aunt Rose coming out of The Regal where they had just seen a film. During the afternoon one of the Air Raid Precaution wardens asked me if I would join the fire watchers. I replied that I would. After tea I went to drill at Sandown station. Before going to bed I wrote to the Air Ministry to inquire about the RAF.

Thursday January 23rd 1941: On my way to Alverstone today I posted the letter I wrote last night. As things are slack at the station I got out the stirrup pump for practice and made a fire of wood, tar, etc. Then, when it was well alight, I squirted water on it. Of course I kept it blazing as long as I could by stopping as soon as it looked like going out!

Friday January 24th 1941: This has been a quiet week for German air raids. This is due, I believe, to the rainy weather.

Saturday January 25th 1941: I bought some British Colonial stamps but, as I started work earlier so that Squibb could go to Portsmouth, I have had no time to sort them out.

Sunday January 26th 1941: On duty this afternoon at Alverstone and it rained all the time. Spent the evening with my stamps.

Monday January 27th 1941: By seven tonight it was still raining hard but, as I had promised to attend an LDV lecture I changed into my uniform and went. Only five members turned up, but I am glad I did for Mr Brown gave us an interesting demonstration on the .300 Lewis gun. It differs slightly from the British .303 as it has no cooling jacket.

Tuesday January 28th 1941: It has been very misty today and, during the afternoon an aeroplane flew over very low but could not be seen on account of it. Later I was told that it was a hostile plane and had machine-gunned Ryde.

Wednesday January 29th 1941: Squibb came early to work today to make up for Saturday. The call up on February 22nd 1941 includes me. Wrote three letters: to Arthur Winter, Aunt Ciss and a schoolmaster in Yorkshire who wanted stamps for his schoolchildren.

Thursday January 30th 1941: I changed over turns of duty at Alverstone today so worked from 1.30pm to 8.30pm. I spoke to Mr Wheway on the telephone to ask him about my joining up. He replied that I must get permission from the Southern Railway Company before I apply for enrolment. Later Edgar came in and we played cards until the last train had passed. On the way home I collided with some silly fool who was walking in the road. I fell off my cycle but was not hurt, neither was the jaywalker. When I got home I found that the glass of my lamp was broken. I wish I had asked his name, then he would have had to buy me a new one.

Friday January 31st 1941: The auditor came to the station but he did not stay long as everything was OK. Wrote to Mr Wheway about my enrolment in the RAF. Returned my .303 rifle to Mr Fowler as we are getting .300 rifles in their place.

Saturday February 1st 1941: Late turn at work today and this morning I rode into Sandown and bought some stamps. Then I was at the station. I finished the January Parcel Accounts. The moon rose early today so it was quite light riding home.

Sunday February 2nd 1941: My Sunday turn of duty at Alverstone. Spent a quiet evening at home.

Monday February 3rd 1941: Letters from the Air Ministry and Aunt Ciss received today. Mr Wheway came out to Alverstone and signed the accounts this afternoon. He told me he was soon going to take over Newport station. I am sorry he is leaving Sandown as he is a decent Station Master.

Tuesday February 4th 1941: It has been very cold again today. Very little has happened since the air raids have slackened.

Wednesday February 5th 1941: I took early turn at Alverstone today and, after tea, I went to Sandown for an LDV lecture. On the way home it was snowing very hard, so I walked, for it was not safe to ride.

Thursday February 6th 1941: Nurse called to see Baby and said that he is getting on very well. He now weighs eight and a half pounds. As the sun came out early the snow had melted by the time I left for Alverstone.

Friday February 7th 1941: I was early turn again today, so Monica and myself went shopping in Sandown during the afternoon.

Saturday February 8th 1941: The reply to my letter to the Southern Railway Company arrived today, giving me permission to join the Armed Forces.

Sunday February 9th 1941: On duty at Alverstone this afternoon, but as it was very slack, I played cards with the boys most of the time. In the evening I wrote to the Officer of Recruiting at Portsmouth to volunteer for the RAF. Heard Churchill's speech – a bit dull and nothing new.

Monday February 10th 1941: The first day of Spring today. Warm and sunny, Monica and myself took Baby for a walk to Alverstone. It was very nice and we all enjoyed it. On the way we saw five swans flying overhead.

Tuesday February 11th 1941: Edgar went over to Portsmouth this morning and, as it was very misty, I wonder if he was delayed at Ryde. A letter arrived in reply to mine of Sunday. It asked me to call at their office in Newport on Friday next. Early this afternoon Monica went out to the Wardens Post to get a gas mask for Baby. Rode into Sandown to get a hair cut and to change my library book. When I got back I had a tiff with Monica because I forgot to get in the coal before I went, but we soon made it up. In the evening we put Baby in his mask and he did not cry a bit.

Wednesday February 12th 1941: It was a very fine morning with a full moon. It was as light as day so, going to Alverstone, I rode from the Waterworks alongside the lane and lit the signal lamp. Squibb is coming before noon on Friday if all goes well. After lunch Monica and myself did a little gardening. Figgaro is not very well, though he was out running about when we were in the garden. He is off his food and I think he has worms. I gave him some olive oil and, tomorrow, must get some powder.

Thursday February 13th 1941: Took late turn at Alverstone today. In the evening Edgar and Marcus came into the station so we had a game of cards. Numerous air raid warnings during the day, of short duration.

Friday February 14th 1941: Today is the day of St Valentine's, Monica gave me a card when I came down to breakfast at 4.30am. As she had kindly packed my suit in a case the night before I was soon on my way to Alverstone. About half past eleven I began to change out of my SR uniform and when Squibb arrived at noon I was all ready. I went to Newport on the 12.11pm train. At the Recruiting Office I only had to wait a short time before seeing the RAF Recruiting Officer. He put me down for flying duties and said they would write to me when I would be required to go over to Portsmouth for a medical examination.

Then I went for a walk around Newport while waiting for the 2.08pm train. First I went to the Post Office and sent a Greetings Telegram to Monica. Next I called at Woolworth's and got some trick floating sugar. As I came out I met Marcus so off we went together. Tried to buy some flower bulbs and a battery for Monica's lamp, but could not. Instead I got for her a bunch of snowdrops and some foreign stamps for myself.

On the way back to the station we met Aunt Rose and Eileen and passed the time of day. I said goodbye to Marcus and returned to Sandown. Told Mr Wheway about the interview before fetching my weekly books from the newsagents. On the way home called in to see Mother. She gave me my birthday present in advance. It is an Ingersoll wristwatch. I really wanted one of these.

Saturday February 15th 1941: One or two of the boys came into St. Nicholas (my home at Lake) this evening and we exchanged a few postage stamps.

Sunday February 16th 1941: It rained most of today so spent the day indoors.

Monday February 17th 1941: Received a letter from the Air Force people asking me to go over to the Portsmouth depot on Friday at 11am. When I got to the station I rang up Mr Wheway and asked him for Friday off. He said I must send him a letter stating the facts and then he would send it into Newport. This I did. Young Mary bought down some stamps and, as I had a few with me, we exchanged them.

Tuesday February 18th 1941: On the way down to the signal to put out the lamp and bring it back to the station for filling I met a frog. He was sitting on a sleeper. It is the first I have seen this year.

Wednesday February 19th 1941: I did not take early turn at Alverstone today as I am having Friday off. Washed my hair when I came home after work.

Thursday February 20th 1941: Had a bath and went early to bed.

Friday February 21st 1941: Went over to Portsmouth at nine this morning, getting there just after ten. On the boat I met another railwayman I met in Newport and we later had tea and lunch together. We went into the Office about eleven and, after filling in some forms, we went to lunch until nearly one. In the afternoon we went through the medical examination. It took over two hours but I passed A1. Then we went in to see the Commanding Officer before leaving. I bought a few foreign stamps before going back to the Island. Monica and Baby were waiting for me at Sandown as she had been shopping.

Saturday 22nd February 1941: This morning I went into Shanklin and asked Mr Times if he had a geometry book he could lend me. He said he was sorry but he did not think he had one. Then I went down to Sandown railway station and saw Mr Wheway. As I had to register for National Service he gave me a paper to take down to the office to say who I was. This I did and returned it to him. Then I went down to the library and got a geometry book and, when I was at Alverstone, young Mary bought me a book of algebra for me to read. On LDV duty 10pm to 6am tonight, the first time since last October. When I arrived at the station I was issued with a Ross rifle number 581, a nine-inch bayonet and 10 rounds of .303 ammunition.

Sunday February 23rd 1941: I am twenty years of age today. In the morning I went to see a fire fighting show on the Fairway. Duty at Alverstone during the afternoon. Mother, Monica and myself had tea together and afterwards played cards. Monica made me a birthday cake with marzipan and four figures for decoration. Monica gave me a Jackdaw fountain pen for a gift and I am writing these words with it.

Monday February 24th 1941: Very high wind today, but it rained little.

Tuesday February 25th 1941: Windy but fair today. During the morning a mine went off at the Home of Rest, damaging a few roof tiles and jammed a door. In the afternoon we took Baby out in his pram. We went into the Battery Gardens and then along the cliff path.

Wednesday February 26th 1941: Bert Jackson rang me up this morning to ask if I would go on LDV guard duty tomorrow night. I said that I would. In the afternoon my cold became worse so I did not go to the LDV lecture, but went early to bed. Monica kindly bought me up a cup of hot milk before I went to sleep.

Thursday February 27th 1941: It rained like hell going to work this morning. I rang up Sandown to tell them I was sorry but, as I had a heavy cold, I could not go out tonight. Went early to bed. By the by, I cut some catkins for Monica.

Friday February 28th 1941: In the afternoon we went shopping in Sandown. I bought a few stamps for my collection.

Saturday March 1st 1941: Did all the Parcels accounts at the station this evening. I had one or two more stamps given to me today.

Sunday March 2nd 1941: In the afternoon we took a walk to Apse Heath and back. The wind was keen but we enjoyed it.

Monday March 3rd 1941: Yesterday Monica and myself took a snap shot of each other holding Baby before we went out in the afternoon. This morning Monica took two more of me in my LDV uniform. At Alverstone I saw a Kingfisher flying along the River Yar.

Tuesday March 4th 1941: On LDV duty again tonight from 10.30pm to 4.30am. During which time there was a good deal of aerial activity and fire bombs were dropped over towards Freshwater. A Police Constable and a Special came down and had a cup of tea. Boyce told us that last night five HEs landed in Brading marshes miles from anywhere. Changed my Ross rifle for a Remington number 290221, which is a .300 calibre.

Wednesday March 5th 1941: As I was out until 4.30 this morning I did late turn at Alverstone.

Thursday March 6th 1941: Lots of toads laying eggs in the ditches around Alverstone.

Friday March 7th 1941: Early turn today, and in the afternoon, Monica and myself went shopping in Sandown. I brought a few stamps home for my collection.

Saturday March 8th 1941: Received a letter from the Air Ministry requesting me to report on March 18th 1941 at Portsmouth and from there to proceed to a Receiving Centre for Attestation. It said I would be away two or three days. I went down and told Mr Wheway about it. While I was on Sandown station an alert sounded and soon after we saw an aeroplane flying very high towards Portsmouth. The AA guns opened fire and it turned in its tracks and flew out to sea. As soon as darkness fell the foe was over again and at about 7.40pm, a very heavy barrage of AA shells with tracer was put up towards Ryde. Mrs Price, who got off the 8.11pm train, said that a plane was brought down into the Solent, but this is very doubtful.

Sunday March 9th 1941: Up early and on an LDV exercise at 9.30am until after 12 noon. Took first guard for an hour. Most people I challenged had left their identity cards at home. By the time 12 came I was fed up and as I had to go to work at 2.30. I came back home. Before I went I took a snapshot of Figgaro the cat and I took another of the boys at Alverstone. As I was writing the first part of today's entry I heard the AA guns in action, so I went outside to watch. Just as I got to the front gate two bombs came whistling down. They landed some way away but I went in and fetched my steel helmet. My luck was OK, for the plane turned out to sea.

Monday March 10th 1941: Report of last night's air attack on Portsmouth. Heavy raid on Portsmouth area and much damage done and losses believed to be heavy. HMS Nelson is in harbour which might have been a target for the foe. Two DL bombs in Ryde, one in Union Lane , the other in a cemetery. One report said four bombs, but two not known. Three dud AA shells landed in Arraton. One hit the road and exploded on impact leaving a small crater which was soon filled in. One German plane was reported shot down. Squibb received his conscription papers and goes for exam on Friday.

Tuesday March 11th 1941: Last night there was another heavy raid on Portsmouth. No reports as yet. Very warm today and, this morning, I caught seven toads which I let go again.

Wednesday March 12th 1941: Started the day by getting up at 8am instead of four because last night I set the clock an hour earlier by mistake. When going up to the Down Distant signal I found a piece of AA shrapnel. On the way back I got some frogs eggs which I hope to hatch into tadpoles. About 11.55am a column of about 50 soldiers halted about 25 yards up the road and then went into our Goods Yard where they had their dinner. On the way home I saw a weasel in Waterworks Lane. Reports of air raid damage done on the night of Monday/Tuesday 10th/ 11th – three people killed when a house was damaged at Shorewell; a Destroyer sunk at Portsmouth and HMS Vernon was badly hit. [HMS Vernon was a land-based Naval training establishment at Portsmouth. German propaganda broadcasts reported it as being 'sunk' on at least one occasion during the war]. The shells that fell on Monday 10th were at Adgestone and not Arraton as reported. Went on LDV duty from 10.30pm to 4.30am. Quiet night with some firing over towards the mainland. During the time three policemen came down for cups of tea. One of them told me about the "invasion barges" which his son is on. These barges are said to have two inch armour plate, a speed of 30 knots, a freeboard of five to six feet and a control turret like a tank. There are three types: assault, transport and tank-carrying. Enough are said to be built to carry 350,000 troops with full supplies.

Thursday March 13th 1941: I was on late turn today so did not get up very early. In the afternoon, while I was at the station, Monica took Baby to the welfare in Sandown. Jack found a dud bomb in Taylor's field. Marcus came down to the station later on and he told me that the cage-like device on Bembridge Fort was a very powerful aircraft detector.

Friday March 14th 1941: It was a very dull and damp day. Monica and myself wrapped up well and took Baby shopping in Sandown. Went back to Alverstone at 6pm.

Saturday March 15th 1941: Quiet day. In the afternoon I went to Sandown and changed my book at the Sandown Free Library. Squibb went for his exam yesterday, that is why I worked overtime.

Sunday March 16th 1941: Monica, Baby and myself went to see the landslip at the Chine, where a good deal of the road has fallen away. On the way home we went into the Tower Gardens and came out by the Old Village, then through the town and back home to tea.

Monday March 17th 1941: Early turn today. Spent today getting ready to go away tomorrow to the RAF Volunteer Reserve depot.

Tuesday March 18th 1941: Left Sandown on the 8.58am train this morning and arrived at the Recruiting Office at Portsmouth about 10.30am. Three others were also on their way to the depot at Uxbridge. I was handed the papers of all four of us, also the tickets for the journey. We left the town station a little after eleven for Waterloo. On the way I wrote two postcards, one for Monica and one for Mother, to say where I was going. I posted them when we arrived in London. One of my companions was called Hugh Chiverton and is Arthur Hookey's nephew. The others came from Southsea and Petersfield. We travelled via Baker Street on the Metropolitan Line and arrived at Uxbridge about 3.30pm. As soon as we had reported to the CO we were issued with knife, fork, spoon and mug. We were given beds and then were told that we were free until nine tomorrow, so we went down for tea. I was so hungry that I had two teas of baked beans on toast. Then we went to the camp cinema and saw a film called "When the Daltons Ride". It was quite good. Later we had supper at the NAAFI and were in bed by nine.

Wednesday March 19th 1941: Up at six this morning, washed, and then had breakfast. Spent the morning passing the educational exams and going before the selection committee. While this was going on there was a gas drill taking place outside. Then we had a break for lunch. I wrote and posted a letter to Mother and Monica telling them how I was getting on. Passed the medical tests in the afternoon and was later enrolled in the RAFVR as Aircraftsman Second Class number 1335461 then Aircraft Hand under training as Air Observer. After tea I went down to the railway station to see about returning home tomorrow. As it was still early I went into a cinema called the Regal where I saw the film Called "Third Finger Left Hand" and went to bed.

Letter dated 19th March 1941 from RAF Uxbridge

Dear Monica,

Well we got here alright at about half past three and, after reporting, had nothing else to do until this morning. Myself and two others spent the evening at the camp cinema and then turned in early to be ready for tomorrow's tests. I passed the educational exams alright and this afternoon go before a Medical Board, so cross your fingers for me. I hope to be home tomorrow at the latest and I send you my love, not forgetting baby Noel, and a pat for Figgaro the cat.

All my love, Leslie.

Thursday March 20th 1941: Up early and arrived home just after twelve. I was very glad to be back again. The stamps I wrote for arrived today and I bought a few of them.

Friday March 21st 1941: Spent the morning in the garden before going to work at half past one. I returned the stamps I did not want and at the same time, ordered more. LDV duty with Mr Mantle from 10.30pm to 4.30am. Johnson did not leave the key of the Guard Room for us so I had to call at his house for it. One PC came down for tea. Very quiet night indeed.

Saturday March 22nd 1941: I did not get up very early today, but just in time to get some more milk from the shop before dinner. Edgar is home on 48 hours leave, and came to see me. He is doing well. Bill came down about seven and we tested the stirrup pump which has just come back after being mended.

Sunday March 23rd 1941: A little colder than of late and it rained a little during the morning. Duty at Alverstone from 2.30pm until 5.30. About half past five, two German bombers came out of low mist, flying North, but they turned back again before coming overhead. The 'pom-poms' opened fire, but nothing else could be seen. An alert was on at the time. Soon after I got home the sound of machine gun fire made me go outside just in time to see a Heinkel 111K dive out of the low cloud, stay in view a few seconds, and then zoom up out of sight once more. Spent the evening mounting a few postage stamps in my collection.

Monday March 24th 1941: When the farmers came down to Alverstone to send off their milk at 7.45 this morning they told me that bombs were dropped on Shanklin yesterday. As Mother had spent last night at Aunt Rose's I was a little worried, so I telephoned to find out if she was alright. Thank God she was safe, but the bombs, two in number, came down only a very short way away. Two houses were destroyed, three people killed, and others hurt. This reminds me, four bombs exploded at Kern farm on Thursday night, but these only made holes in a field.

Tuesday March 25th 1941: Spent this afternoon in the garden. Did quite a lot of digging and planted the rest of the shallots. At noon today Yugoslavia joined the three power pact. Today is Greek independence day, and, as they are the only people in the Balkans brave enough to defy the foe, God stand by them to give them victory.

Wednesday March 26th 1941: It rained all day today, so have to spend the afternoon indoors.

Thursday March 27th 1941: Late turn of duty at Alverstone today. Good News: the Yugoslav people have overthrown the Government and put young King Peter II on the throne, pray God be behind him and all who are true to their country. I was so pleased to hear this over the radio, I rode down to Sandown to tell Mother. While I was there we heard machine guns in action. We went into the Ocean Hotel and, on looking out of the window, we saw the gunners firing at a black object bobbing in the water. It might have been a mine, but I could not wait to see for I was already late.

Friday March 28th 1941: Got my books today, but this is the last issue of *Modern Wonder* and *The War* is only being issued fortnightly now. On LDV duty from 10.30pm to 4.30am. It rained most of the night and no aircraft were about.

Saturday March 29th 1941: My new LDV uniform came out on the 8.26am train this morning. It is size 8 and fits fairly well. The stamps I ordered have not yet arrived.

Sunday March 30th 1941: Yesterday I got a nose cap of an AA shell. Today we walked into Shanklin to see the damage done last Sunday. Two houses were destroyed and Green Lane blocked to traffic. Came back along Landguard Road. The wind was rather cold but we both enjoyed it.

Monday March 31st 1941: Very cold wind today. Planted two rows of French Beans, one of peas and three of parsnips in the garden. They are all last year's seeds, so I hope they come up alright.

Tuesday April 1st 1941: All Fools Day, but people were too busy to uphold it. Even the children seemed to have forgotten it. This is the first day that I have not needed to light the signal lamps for daylight for about 6am until after 8am. Bill and Marcus walked as far as Waterworks lane with me on the way home.

Wednesday April 2nd 1941: I was on early turn at Alverstone today. In the afternoon Monica and myself took Baby for a walk along the cliff to Shanklin and back. I was quite ready for tea by the time we got home.

Thursday April 3rd 1941: Johnson rang me up on the telephone this afternoon to remind me it was my turn of LDV duty tomorrow.

Friday April 4th 1941: I had such a headache when I came home from Alverstone this evening that I could not go out on LDV duty. Monica, like a dear, went round and told Mr Mantle that I would not be out tonight.

Saturday April 5th 1941: I did not feel very well when I returned home after work. I think that I have a touch of 'flu.

Sunday April 6th 1941: Spent the day in bed, Monica kindly went out and telephoned to Sandown station to say that I was unwell, so could not go to Alverstone today. Felt much better after a sleep in the afternoon.

Monday April 7th 1941: I felt much better this morning so went along to Sandown and saw the Station Master. I told him I would go to work as usual this afternoon. Which I did.

Tuesday April 8th 1941: Monica bought some pea, turnip, lettuce and beetroot seeds. Mr Lewis lent me Hall and Knight's Elementary Algebra, so I can study logarithms.

Wednesday April 9th 1941: Early turn today. Arthur, from the mill, told about the German incendiary bombs dropped around Newchurch about 11pm last night; no damage reported. Young Brimstone took Squibb's place today as Squibb has gone up to Oxford. Spent the afternoon gardening.

Thursday April 10th 1941: Went shopping in Sandown with Monica this afternoon. Got my weekly books from the newsagents. Monica bought Baby a rattle. Heavy firing tonight. I should not be surprised if bombs were dropped near home.

Friday April 11th 1941: Soon after I arrived at Alverstone, Arthur Hookey came in, to say that a bomb had landed around the Lynch. He had been on guard at the Waterworks during the night, and had seen a German bomber shot down in flames over towards Godshill. After the goods train had passed I walked down the line to Burnt House, and then across the marsh to the Lynch, but I saw no sign of the crater the bomb must have made. As I was returning past Alverstone Farm I saw Mr Plumbley in his field. The two bombs had exploded within ten yards of the crater that the old bomb made. Jack and Mrs Orchard came over to see them, but the holes were very small. Later Marcus came down and gave me a nose cap of another AA shell that he had found. He also told me that two DLs were in the marsh so we went down to see. We fiddled about down there for a time but we could not make up our minds whether they had gone off, or not. We arranged to go for a cycle ride in the afternoon.

Marcus called for me a little after three and we rode into Shanklin to see the bomb damage done in Green Lane. Met Mr and Mrs Beddow and they asked how Monica and Baby were getting on. Leaving them we rode to Godshill and after much enquiring, we at last found the wreckage of the German aircraft about six miles further on. It was still smouldering in places. In the fuselage were two "things" that once had been men, but, when we saw them, they looked scarcely human. I will not try to describe them for the sight sickened me, while the stench of burning flesh was terrible. The guard told us that the plane had been burning all day. I picked up four pieces as souvenirs. For a mile or so on the way home we neither spoke for they were the first men we both had seen killed in action. Said "So long" to Marcus at Apse Heath and returned home for tea. Just before leaving home about ten to go on guard at Sandown station, I heard a shell go flying over. I did not hear any explosion.

When I got to the station I found out that the shell had landed in the Newport line near the Signal Box. The Station Master came down to see if any damage had been done and three policemen also arrived on the scene. After a time they all went home and left Mr Mantle and myself to finish our watch. Heavy raid on Portsmouth but did not last long. Came off duty a little before four.

Saturday April 12th 1941: Because of the AA shell at Sandown station the "push and pull" train ran between Merstone and Sandown. Squibb came back today and told me that he had failed to pass the tests for flying service so they have put him on the ground staff for general duties.

Sunday April 13th 1941: Went for a walk in the country, taking Baby with us. It was a bit of a job getting his pram over the gates and styles but we managed it. Met the boys from Alverstone and they all looked at Baby and he smiled at them.

Monday April 14th 1941: Started to cut the front lawn this morning but it began to rain before I had time to finish it. Edgar was home on a short leave today so he came in to see me.

Tuesday April 15th 1941: Lovely sunny day. Monica said that as my holidays start next Monday we might be able to go to Rye, so I am getting tickets to take us there.

Wednesday April 16th 1941: Finished cutting the lawn and trimming the edges this morning„ It has been another lovely day and, at Alverstone, quite a number of people have been out picking flowers. At tea time Marcus and myself went fishing, with Edgar's rod, up by Black Rock bridge. Two of the children from Sandown missed the 5.20 train and rather than walk and lose the use of their tickets, they waited two hours for the next train.

Thursday April 17th 1941: The railway passes for Monica and myself arrived today. Very heavy air raid on Portsmouth lasting nearly all the night. I expect the loss of life must be on the heavy side. There was a mobile AA gun not far from home and it made the place shake every time it fired.

Friday April 18th 1941: It rained most of today. On LDV duty 10.30pm to 4.30am but, as it was still raining, and no "warning" sounded, we stayed in our hut.

Saturday April 19th 1941: This morning I took a suitcase, that Monica had packed with some of our kit, to the railway station, and sent it off to Rye. While I was there I got the Station Master to sign four privilege ticket orders. Very little to note in the afternoon.

Sunday April 20th 1941: Spent most of today, except while I was at work, getting ready for going away tomorrow morning, if all goes well.

Monday April 21st 1941: Monica, Baby and myself left Sandown at 11.25am bound for Rye. The crossing to the mainland was very nice as it was quite warm. We travelled via Portsmouth, Brighton and Hastings. It was a little difficult crossing Portsmouth as the roads are so much blown up by bombs. A boy took our luggage to the town station. We just had time to catch the Hastings train at Brighton. When we arrived at Hastings we had time for a cup of tea before going on. Nora met us at the station, and so did a policeman, who wanted to know what we were doing in a defence area. We told him, but he was a bit doubtful if we could stay, but he let us pass. After tea Monica, and myself, went out for a short walk round. While we were gone the policeman came down and told Nora that we could stay. Before I end today I must say that Baby was very good travelling.

Tuesday April 22nd 1941: Went into Rye this morning and sent a card home to Mother. Then we went into the Church to see the pendulum of the clock, which hangs down through the roof into the building. Next we walked to the old gateway called "The Land Gate". It is a part of the old town wall. After tea we went to the Regent cinema and saw a film called "The return of Frank James". It was very good indeed.

Wednesday April 23rd 1941: Today Monica and myself left Baby with Nora, and took a train to Sittingbourne. We went via

Ashford and Canterbury. When we arrived at Canterbury East we had nearly two hours to spare before the one to Sittingbourne left the West railway station. Then we looked over a museum, and saw an old gateway in what was the old wall. Next I bought a few postage stamps for my collection. We saw part of the Cathedral, and the tomb of the Black Prince, before we left the city. On arriving at Sittingbourne we had lunch and then walked into Milton Regis. We visited some of Monica's friends and had tea with one of them. Bought some dog biscuits for Auntie's dog and bean seeds, from a Mrs Bates, whom Monica stayed with at one time. She kindly gave us some cabbage and turnip seeds. We were a little late in leaving for the station so the Manager of the Gas Works gave us a lift in his car. He need not have bothered, for the train was forty minutes late, so we missed the connection at Canterbury. It was over an hour before we left this latter station. In the meantime we had a cup of tea and a bun or two in the buffet. We were very tired before we got back to Rye.

Thursday April 24th 1941: Up late, and spent the morning reading. A German aircraft was brought down at Camber about 10am. I heard it going down, but did not see it. Camber is only about three miles from Rye. In the afternoon we went shopping and bought a spoon with a crest of Rye on it for Mother, After tea we went again to the films and saw 'Strike Up the Band'. It was quite good.

> *Letter dated April 24th 1941: from Los Angeles, California, USA*
>
> *Dear Leslie,*
>
> *Many thanks for your very welcome letter dated January 29th, which I received today. I can't tell you how glad I was to get it, and to know that you and your dear Mother are safe. The British Societies here are all working hard to raise funds for England. All the Ladies of these societies*

are either sewing or knitting. The group I belong to are knitting stockings for children and making hospital garments. Our favourite song is "There will always be an England".

I am proud to hear you say you hope to join the RAF dear, but why not stay in the Home Guard a little longer. You know you are all your Mother has. How does she feel about it? After all, you are only just twenty.

Well dear, we have had a terrible rainy period. It has rained almost continually for four weeks and the streets are like rivers. Although today the sun is shining there has been a great amount of damage done by the floods. I pray that this terrible war will soon be over. Good night and God bless you both. Love from all.

Aunt Ciss

Friday April 25th 1941: Very cold, so we did not go out very much but we did go to see the Old Tower. The museum there was closed so I could not look over it. Wrote a letter to Mother. In the afternoon we went to see Winnie, but she was out.

Saturday April 26th 1941: Took one of our bags round to the station to have it sent back to Sandown, also posted a card to Mother. Called again to see Winnie, and this time she was in. She came back to Nora's with us for tea. Later we saw her back to her home. Bought a few more postage stamps for my collection.

Sunday April 27th 1941: The train was late leaving Rye this morning and so we missed the connection at Brighton. The next did not leave until 1.15pm and arrived at Portsmouth Town station about 2.50pm. We had a cup of tea and came over on the 4.30pm boat and arrived home about half past six. After tea I rang up Mother at Shanklin to see that she was all right.

Monday April 28th 1941: Went into Sandown to see Mother and gave her our gift from Rye. I was told that on Thursday April 24th German aircraft dropped hundreds of incendiary bombs around the Island. Very little damage was dons, but four people were killed at Cowes.

Tuesday April 29th 1941: I went on the 12.6 train to Alverstone so that Squibb could get away to catch a train as he is going away for two days.

Wednesday 30th April 1941: Young Brimstone took Squibb's place today. As it is the last day of the month I spent the afternoon cashing up and filling up weekly forms. Found time to go boating on the river for half an hour or so.

Thursday May 1st 1941: Started the monthly accounts today. Had a fire fighting practice in the evening.

Friday May 2nd 1941: May day, and it rained all morning. Finished the accounts. Sandown rang me up to say that it was my turn for LDV guard tonight. Went shopping with Monica this afternoon and got some more postage stamps for my albums.

Saturday May 3rd 1941: Monica brought up my breakfast in bed for me this morning, so I was not up very early. Late duty today, but nothing about it is worthy to note. I must not forget to put the other hour on the clock tonight. Monica got two oranges this afternoon, the first we have seen for months.

Sunday May 4th 1941: Did no gardening before breakfast, but afterwards I did quite a lot of digging. Afternoon I spent on duty at Alverstone.

Monday May 5th 1941: Early turn this morning and, while we were having breakfast, the A.A. guns were in action. Riding along early it was very cold as the clock is now two hours ahead of Greenwich mean time. The new train service began today, but no more passengers travelled.

Tuesday May 6th 1941: The all clear did not go until after five this morning. As yesterday I came back home on the 1.31pm train. In the afternoon went shopping with Monica in Shanklin. While I was there I bought ten stamps of Guatemala for sixpence. Four of them, I found later, I had already got. I also bought a 13 cent blue Canadian stamp for four pence.

Wednesday May 7th 1941: Spent most of the afternoon in the garden. The French beans, turnips and peas are all coming up very yell. I still have quite a lot of ground to dig.

Thursday May 8th 1941: Monica and myself went to Sandown this evening. After leaving Baby With Mother we saw the film 'Spring Parade' at the Queens. It was very good indeed. While we were in the shop Polly came in to see Noel. She is in the ATS now and is stationed at Yaverland. Mother said that late last night Eileen was taken to the Home of Rest hospital in an ambulance. There she underwent an operation for appendicitis, but everything went off well and she is getting over it now. Mother took Baby along to Shanklin, to Aunt Rose's, and did not get back home again until nearly ten. On LDV duty 10.30pm to 4am.

Friday May 9th 1941: In the afternoon Monica and myself went shopping in Sandown. Bought a few stamps to add to my collection.

Saturday May 10th 1941: Spent the afternoon gardening. The ground is very dry and we could do with some rain. Bombs fell at about 12pm.

Sunday May 11th 1941: Took a walk to Brading during the afternoon and, as it was a fine day, we enjoyed it very much. We went over the church and saw the tombs of two Elizabethan Knights. We returned by train, getting home in nice time for tea. As we were undressing for bed a little before midnight we heard a series of explosions in the direction of Newport, but only a mile or so away from us.

Monday May 12th 1941: On Saturday sixteen small bombs fell around Hill Top and Queen's Bower. No damage done except a few windows broken. Four more fell near to the railway line not far up from Alverstone, on Sunday night. During Saturday afternoon the gorse took fire on the golf links. It took some time to put out. A baby calf was born in the field behind the station. It is a funny little thing.

Tuesday May 13th 1941: Spent this morning in the garden. Cut the hedge and generally tidying up. Afternoon fine and warm but not quite warm enough for Spring.

Wednesday May 14th 1941: Early turn today, and, after tea, we went to Shanklin. Left Baby with Mother at Auntie's while we went to the Regal. The film was called 'Brigham Young'. It was about the Mormons and was a fine show. I got 6/1 [six shillings and a penny] for some stamps that I sold.

Thursday May 15th 1941: This morning I rode into Sandown and bought 12 good Colonial stamps for 4/6 [four shillings and sixpence].

Friday May 16th 1941: Very heavy frost before we got up this morning. Very little else to note.

Saturday May 17th 1941: Baby woke up about four this morning and cried for a bottle, so I went down to fill one. While

I was down in the kitchen a German aircraft flew very low overhead, making for its base. The searchlights were on, but no guns fired. Washed the windows after breakfast.

Sunday May 18th 1941: A very nice day again, warm and sunny. Duty in the afternoon at Alverstone from 2.30 to 5.20pm. Spent the evening with my books and writing and drawing as it pleased me. Now I must drink my coffee and make ready to go on LDV guard by 10.30pm.

Monday May 19th 1941: Came off guard at four this morning after a quiet and uneventful night. Arrived at Alverstone just before six. The goods train was over half an hour late because Len overslept and did not get to Merstone on time. While I was eating my second breakfast a little brown mouse ran out from under the safe and began to eat the crumbs that I had dropped. Took this afternoon easy because I was still tired from last night. As I write this Baby is laying in his cradle playing with his fingers and laughing every time I catch his eye. He is a dear funny little chap who always cries for more when his bottle comes to an end, but he soon falls asleep. He kicks all his bed clothes off and then pulls them over his head for a change. If he is in a good humour he will play Peep-Bo with his bib. So Good Night baby Noel, its time for you to go to sleep. Early this morning saw ten aircraft flying in box formation of six and four planes. I took them to be English though someone did say that they were hostile. During the nine o'clock news it was stated that ten Messerschmitt 109s were over the south coast. Five were destroyed by RAF planes, when attacking shipping in the Channel. Two English machines were lost.

Tuesday May 20th 1941: Weeded the French beans this morning and set fire to the rubbish which has accumulated. Before lunch I went round to Woodhams shop to fetch the weekly groceries. Vic killed an adder in Mrs Allen's garden. It was only a small one.

Wednesday May 21st 1941: Watched a Blackbird dropping worms down one of the chimneys at the station. I climbed up onto the roof and found a nest full of young fledglings. Just before four this afternoon I received a letter from the Officer in charge of Records at Wantage Hall, Reading, requiring me to report at Stratford on Avon on the 31st of May 1941 before 6pm. I did not expect to go just yet, but there it is, and so we must make the best of it. Hope everything is OK there and Monica is alright without me to look after her. I went along to Sandown station to tell the Station Master that I will be leaving the Railway soon. He said that he would try to get me two days free from work next week.

Thursday May 22nd 1941: A wet miserable sort of day. After lunch Monica and myself, not forgetting Baby, went shopping in Sandown. I bought eleven more stamps for my collection; they cost me two shillings. Quite a number of people wished me luck when I leave for the RAF.

Friday May 23rd 1941: It has not been a very nice day. The rain fell for a short while in the afternoon, but it cleared up towards the twilight. Mother looked after Baby so that Monica and myself could go to the Rivoli. The film was called 'The Thief of Baghdad'. It was excellent. One of the very best I have ever seen.

Saturday May 24th 1941: Rained most of the day. By noon it was falling very heavily. A little before eight a German aircraft flew at a very high speed over Lake with the AA guns firing on it. When it had passed overhead, and was about half a mile away, machine guns went into action. Whether it was our ground defence guns, or the Germans, I do not know.

Sunday May 25th 1941: Did not get up until after ten, and by the time we had breakfast and I had bathed, it was dinner time.

We had a special dinner for it is the last that I will have at home for some while. It was pork, potatoes and cauliflower, with tinned grapefruit and cream, which Monica had been saving up for some time, for dessert. After tea we played draughts and listened to the radio until bed time. Dinner was lovely.

Monday May 26th 1941: Early on Saturday evening hostile aircraft bombed the area North of Newport around the cement works. They damaged the railroad so that a Down train was derailed. Luckily the engine, and carriages kept on an even keel. Three people were injured. It rained very hard for most of the day. Young John Duff came out from Ventnor West to be taught the work at Alverstone. In the afternoon the Station Master was out, and gave me more forms to be filled in when I join up. They are about making my RAF pay up to Railway pay.

Tuesday May 27th 1941: Last night bombs hit Northwood cemetery, blowing open a number of graves. No other damage reported. Duff did late turn with me today so that I could show him how to lock up the station and crossing gates. I found a Thrush's nest, but, as the bird was on the nest, I could not see the eggs. Four Cygnets were born at the Waterworks. Edgar came home on seven days leave. I start my two days holiday tomorrow. Oh dear; I do not want to go away from home and everything I am fond of. Still, I must not shirk my duty.

Wednesday May 28th 1941: Northwood was bombed again early this morning. No damage. In the afternoon Monica and myself were in the garden. Cut the lawn, weeded the peas, planted two rows of runner beans and dug a little. Tried to light a bonfire but the paper must have been wet for it would not light. After tea we played a game called 'Lets go Shopping' and then played cards until supper time.

Thursday May 29th 1941: We did not get up very early this morning for it is the last day on which I will get a chance for some little time. In the afternoon we went shopping in Sandown after I had been to the station to collect my pay. Got a number of articles to take away with me, such as writing paper, stamps and notebooks. After tea Mr Mantle same round and I handed over my LDV equipment for him to take back for me.

Friday May 30th 1941: Last day at Alverstone station before I go away. A number of people wished me Good Luck in the RAF. In the afternoon went to Sandown and bought two RAF broochs, one for Monica and the other for Mother. While I was there I fetched my books from the newsagents. After tea we packed my things and Mr Mantle came round to say So Long. Had a bath, a cup of coffee, and so to bed. As I leave at 8.5am for Sandown this will be the last entry is this journal for some time. While I am with the RAF I will write in a small pocket book. So, for a time, Goodbye.

Saturday July 19th 1941: Written when I returned home on leave after having been some seven weeks in the RAF. The following is re-written from my small diary, carried at the time:-

Saturday May 31st 1941: at the Shakespeare Hotel, Stratford upon Avon. Left Sandown at 8.58am by train. Monica, Mother and Baby came to see me off. I was very sad at leaving, but hope to be back with them soon. On the way over from the Island to Portsmouth I saw a number of small naval craft coming out of the harbour entrance. The first was throwing oil out onto the water while a second, slightly larger, was towing 27 mines. The journey up to London was uneventful and after having lunch at a place near to Paddington, I went on to the station. The train up to Leamington Spa was packed, for a large number of

Londoners were off to see their children over the weekend. Arrived a little late at Stratford, but so did a lot of other recruits. Made friends with a tall chap called Allen Vaughn, who I met on the train. First we went and filled in more forms and then we had tea. Later four of us went rowing on the river Avon until nearly nine, when we returned to the hotel. Wrote a letter to Monica and then turned in.

Letter dated Sat May 31st 1941 from No.1335461 Aircraftsman Second Class Harris L. at Stratford.

My Dearest Wife,

Arrived here safely and have nice quarters in an hotel. Four of us went rowing an the river until nearly nine. Tomorrow we are to be measured for our uniforms. This is just a line or so to say that I am alright. I do hope that you do not miss me too much.

My love to you dear, to Baby, Mother and Figgaro the cat.

Your loving husband Leslie.

Sunday June 1st 1941: Up by 7.15am, then a wash, followed by breakfast of corn flakes and sausages. At 0850hrs we went down to the store and were issued with our kit. Back we carried the lot and next went to the tailor to be fitted for our uniforms. As some alterations are to be made I have to wait a week before I can wear them. We were addressed by the Commanding Officer and the Medical Officer, at the Shakespeare Theatre. Then dinner, after which we three (Allen, George and myself) went for a stroll around Stratford. We returned for tea and, later walked to the railway station, during which time I posted the two letters home that I wrote this morning. After supper at 19.30hrs, the three of us went out on the river. The others rowed as I have blisters on my hands from Saturday's boating expedition. I do miss home, Monica, Mother and everything, in fact. Well, now for bed.

*Letter dated June 1st 1941 from AC2 L. Harris at
Stratford on Avon.*

Dearest Monica,

*I am sitting by the river watching people boating as I
cannot row today for I have blisters on my hands from
boating yesterday. Real ones this time, not imaginary ones
like I got when gardening. We are likely to stay at
Stratford for about two days or so. We only come here to
be equipped with our kit before being posted to another
unit. I have heard it said that we might be sent to
Torquay, but nothing official yet. I hope we do go there for
it will be nearer home and much easier for you to join
me.*

*The journey up from Paddington was rotten. There were
sixteen of us in a compartment only meant to hold, eight,
so you can imagine the crush. When the tailor has
finished the alterations to my uniforms I hope I can send
you a photograph of myself. Well., love, it is nearly four, so
I must go back for tea.*

All my love to you, darling wife, Leslie.

Monday June 2nd 1941: This morning we were lectured by
the Education Officer. Next we were photographed for our
identity cards and later, we were vaccinated and inoculated, so
we have 48 hours off. Just before 11.00hrs we filled in forms for
our pay and marriage allowance. By 16.00hrs my arm began to
hurt a little. Spent most of the afternoon fixing my equipment.

Tuesday June 3rd 1941: Rest day today after yesterdays
inoculation. Went shopping in the morning for some cleaning
kit. Spent the afternoon sleeping and writing home. After tea
three of us went for a walk before turning in for the night. We
went a very nice way across country. On the way we passed
through an avenue of trees and saw no less than three grey
squirrels playing in the branches.

Letter dated June 3rd 1941, from AC2 L. Harris at Stratford on Avon.

Sweetheart,

Well darling, how are things getting along at home? I hope that Baby is being very good and that Figgaro is behaving himself in the garden. We were inoculated on Monday then given 48 hours off to get over the effects. My room mates, George and Allen and myself, went shopping for some cleaning kit for our uniform buttons, which are brass and will need cleaning every day. Have you heard about the new clothes ration? I did not hear of it until this morning as we have been unable to get a newspaper. I do not think there is a radio in the building so, if you are in and listen to The Island in the Mist *on Wednesday, do not forget to tell me all about it. Our corporal, who is decent chap, said that your allowances should be through soon, so let me know about it when it arrives. This evening I am thinking of walking along to the old church, and see the tomb of Shakespeare. Well, love, it is nearly tea time again so I must end this letter.*

All my love to you and Baby, Leslie.

Wednesday June 4th 1941: Squad drill from 11.30 to 12.30hrs, when it was time for dinner. A lecture in the afternoon followed by more drill before tea. Afterwards we received all our uniform except the greatcoat. We went out to the canteen before supper. Later I helped with supper and got a double helping for doing so. I spent the time before lights out polishing buttons and boots. At tea I received a letter from Monica.

Thursday June 5th 1941: Went to the Lecture Hall this morning but as the Education Officer did not turn up we came back again. On the way it began to rain quite hard. We expect to leave here on Saturday. Drill again in the afternoon, followed by a lecture by the Medical Officer. In the evening a party of us saw the play King Richard the Third at the Shakespeare Theatre. I did enjoy it.

Letter dated June 5th 1941, *from AC2 L. Harris at Stratford on Avon.*

Dearest Monica,

Your letter arrived last night and I read it before turning in. It is raining like the devil outside so there will not be any drill today, thank goodness. Baby must look jolly making the water fly while he is in his bath. The Laburnum trees must look very nice in their yellow jackets now. I have only seen one of them in Stratford, and that was in a park. Two fellows fell in the river, and had to go to bed yesterday. Luckily their uniforms were ready this morning. I have my uniform now and spend most of my spare time polishing the buttons. I sat my first mathematics examination this morning. I think I got on quite well. I do believe we are leaving Stratford on Saturday, but, as yet, have no idea where we are off to.

About twenty of us are going with the corporal to see the play King Richard the Third tonight. We get in for one and threepence and sit in the seven and six seats if we go in a party. Not bad is it? As it is nearly half past one I must go on parade in five minutes so I will continue this letter later. It is just 5.20pm and we have finished for today. We have been busy all afternoon. First we went to the Gas Chamber and, after having put on our gas masks, we passed through the place. Just before we came out we had to take our masks off so that we got a whiff of the stuff. It made tears run down my cheeks, but, on going outside, the wind quickly blew it away. We have sheets on our beds which is something that the Army does not get. We are well looked after as at every meal an Officer comes round to ask if any one has any complaints. So far not one of us has. "Let me tell you" I eat up carrots and cabbage at dinner time because I was so hungry. Can you

get me from Sandown, four cloth Volunteer Reserve
badges for my uniforms. The shops here have run out due
to the large number of recruits passing through. I got my
identity card today. The fatheads have put my height as
five foot ten so I must have grown quickly! Well,
sweetheart, I must polish my shoes before going off with
the rest of the flight to see the play.

With all my love, your loving husband, Leslie.

Friday June 6th 1941: The CO gave us an inspection this morning, but, as it was raining at the time, it did not last long. I had a haircut and shampoo afterwards. Later the Education Officer gave us an address on behalf of the CO who was unable to be present. We leave tomorrow for St. Andrews in Scotland. I am to be in G Flight of 12 Initial Training Wing. I received a parcel from Monica and a letter from Mother. I replied to both and also sent Monica the ten shillings pay that I got today. After tea I went to The Picture House and saw a film called 'The Mask of Zorro'. It was very good indeed. I packed my kitbag ready for going away tomorrow and then turned in for bed.

Letter dated June 6th 1941, *Stratford on Avon.*

My love,

I must catch the post, so will not write much. Thanks for
the food parcel, it will do us well on the journey to
Scotland tomorrow. I passed the maths exam OK and now
have the privilege of wearing a white flash in my cap. I
am sending ten shillings to help you and Baby along. I
will let you know my next address as soon as possible. I
must hurry to the Post Office.

Love to you both from Leslie.

Saturday June 7th 1941: Took a last walk around Stratford with Allen Vaughn and George Fox, before leaving. We went into the canteen and had a cup of tea. Then we played a few games of table tennis before dinner. I also slipped down to the church to see Shakspeare's tomb. There is no name on it, but a tablet is set into the nearby wall. After dinner we loaded our kit bags into a waiting lorry. We had to travel in our skeleton webbing which consisted of a full water bottle and haversack, containing small items. We also put on greatcoats and had to carry gas masks and our steel helmets. We then marched to the Washington Irving Hotel, where we had tea. Flights F, G and H of 12 ITW entrained at 17.30hrs at the London, Midland and Scottish station. Before we left we made a gift of sixpence each to our old NCO, Corporal Lanning. He was a very nice fellow.

On the train we had plenty of room as we were only six to each compartment. At Leicester we all had a cup of tea and a sandwich. We left there about 19.40hrs on over the river Trent and to Nottingham, where we saw the castle up on the hill. On past the pit heads of coal mines, and out again into open country. On sped the train via Newcastle and Edinburgh and at last arrived at St Andrews by 07.30hrs on Sunday morning.

Sunday June 8th 1941: The Imperial Hotel, St Andrews, Fifeshire. After detraining we marched to the Imperial Hotel, where we had breakfast. Later the C.O. gave us an address of welcome. From then until dinner time we were filling in forms and things. We were then free at 2pm and so spent the rest of the day writing home, and looking round the town. It is not much of a town with few shops. To bed early as we get up at six tomorrow morning.

Letter dated June 8th 1941, *St Andrews.*

My darling wife,

I arrived here at half past seven after an all night journey of some sixteen hours. Of course, we did not travel on main lines, but by round about ways. We left Stratford just after half past five in the evening. At 7.20 we stopped for tea at Leicester and by 8.30 the train was running to Nottingham. York was the next stopping place, where we had 15 minutes to walk on the platform. This was at 11.15. On through the night to Newcastle at 1am and Berwick at about 4am. I had been asleep since we left York, but I woke to see us passing through Edinburgh, Over the Forth Bridge ran the train and into St Andrews at 7.30am.

We have quite nice billets in the Imperial Hotel. We are three to a room which come complete with hot and cold running water. Luckily Allen, George and myself were able to get a room together.

This is a new training wing and our Squadron Leader is the Earl of Haddington. He gave us a welcoming address and told us that he wanted this new squadron to be the very best in the RAF and that we all must work very hard to make it so.

We would have classes and some drill during the day and also evening classes several nights each week, so you can see that I am not going to get much spare time. We are here for only six weeks and those successful will get seven days leave before moving South to another training school. We can then spend some time together. I will send you some of my pay each fortnight, for travelling expenses, if that is necessary. I do hope you have not had any air raids since I have been away, or any other worries. I hope that baby Noel is growing well.

With all my love to you and Noel. Leslie

Monday June 9th 1941: 06.00 Reveille. 06.45 Breakfast. 08.00 to 10.00 Maths. I got 76 marks at Stratford. 11.00 to 12.00 Morse code. 12.00 to 12.30 Anti gas precautions. 12.30 to 13.30 Lunch. 13.30 to 16.30 Parade and drill. 16.30 to 18.00 break. After tea the three of us went to the Picture House to see a film called 'Kit Carson'. The film was good but the talking apparatus in the cinema was very poor. Afterwards we had a cup of tea at the YMCA before returning to bed. At the YMCA, two Poles were playing chess. How they could concentrate with so much noise around them I do not know.

Tuesday June 10th 1941: Signalling and maths this morning. It is very cold here early in the day, but it gets very warm when the sun comes out. On Fire Picket this night, but, as there was no warning, did not have to get up.

Wednesday June 11th 1941: Lessons as usual and, during the morning. I was inoculated, so I did not feel like going out this evening. I received a letter from Monica, which I answered, and wrote one to Mother before going to bed.

> *June 11th 1941 letter from AC2 L. Harris* at St
> Andrews.
>
> *My beloved,*
>
> *Received your letter dated the 5th this afternoon, it had been sent on from Stratford. It was good to hear that you and Baby are both doing well. We have been lucky again with our NCO. This time he is a Sergeant called Last and is a very fine man indeed. He is only about five feet six inches tall, but what he lacks in inches he makes up in spirit. Last night six of us were on Fire Picket and before we turned in he came round with cups of tea and sandwiches. Then he made our beds for us in a way he called a 'Flea Bag', and very warm it was too. We had our third inoculation today so we all turned in early,*

*supposedly suffering after effects, but actually to avoid
extra guard duty as the Old Man has said that anyone fit
enough was to replace those feeling unwell. We have all
learnt what 'swinging the lead' means!*

*Two of the chaps were really ill at tea time and our
sergeant took their tea up to their rooms, he is that kind of
a man. It is funny I should be writing about him just then
for he has just been in with a big bottle of aspirins, in case
we had headaches. We took two each, not because we
needed them, but in ease he suggested that we went out on
guard. Our sergeant is married, but his family must be
somewhere else, as he has his own room just along the
corridor, from us. Our Flight Commander was a barrister
in civil life and he has a dry sort of humour which often
makes us laugh. Naturally he lectures us on Air Force law
and Kings Regulations and is able to make a dry subject
very interesting indeed.*

*Last night, when I was in the YMCA, I played a game of
chess with a Polish soldier. He could not speak any
English and, when I went in, he was sitting at the board,
fingering the pieces. I went over and looked at the board.
He saw me, smiled and pointed first to the board and then
to me. I nodded to say that I could play and he pulled out
a chair for me. During the game I managed to take one of
his Knights and he said something like 'Kerrizot'. I did not
know if he was congratulating me, or swearing at me! He
won in the end and, before I went he got me a cup of tea
and shook my hand.*

*The cooks and kitchen staff here are all civilians and, as
we are in Scotland, we have porridge with our breakfast,
which I do not like, so this morning I put my porridge to
one side and began eating the bacon and beans that we
had as our second course. At that moment the cook, a big
burly Scot well over six feet tall, came out of the kitchen
and, seeing that I had left my porridge, asked me why. I
said that I did not like it without milk and sugar. He said*

that I would spoil its flavour that way and, grabbing the salt cellar from the table, poured a large amount into the porridge, stirring it in with a spoon. "Now try that," he suggested, "it will make a man of you and double the size of your muscles!" So I had to eat it and then handed my empty plate to the cook. He grinned, and said that tomorrow he would make sure that I got an extra helping. Still, it did not taste too bad and I can always hope that he is on a different turn of duty next day.

Well dear, it is time for bed, so I must end now.

Your loving husband, Leslie.

Thursday June 12th 1941: Lessons much as usual and nothing else to note.

Friday June 13th 1941: Played golf on the New St Andrews course. I did 10 holes in 100 strokes during the afternoon.

Saturday June 14th 1941: Finished lectures at 1230hrs and, after lunch, three of us went for a game of golf. As tea is earlier on Saturday we only played six holes. Wrote letters home on the seafront in the evening until it began to rain when I went into the YMCA and finished them. A parcel arrived from Monica and letters from Mother and young Mary Barwell at Alverstone.

Sunday June 15th 1941: Church parade at 0830hrs. The rest of the day we had to ourselves, but have little to do but write letters home. Also put my lecture notes in order.

Letter dated June 15th 1941 – *St. Andrews.*

My precious darling,

I received your parcel containing all those nice things yesterday morning. I am pleased to know you are getting on fairly well without me but I am so looking forward to my next leave. My room mates also got food parcels so we shared and made a very good supper, especially as tea is earlier at weekends. It is very nice of you to send things but you must not use up all your ration points for me as you have yourself and baby to feed.

After all, the food is not too bad here. It is nice to be by the sea again. The bay is nearly 20 miles wide and beyond can be seen range after range of hills, stretching away for over 100 miles. Above them all rise blue mountains, snow capped even though it is now June. I was told they are over 3,400 feet high. Friday afternoon is Organised Games time so I opted to play golf, together with one of my pals. The Wing Commander very kindly lent us his clubs. I believe he thought that we could really play golf. The golf links are free to any cadet from the Initial Training Wing, so we had nothing to pay. I enjoyed myself very much, even if quite a lot of time was spent looking for lost balls. We were very careful with the clubs as they were good ones. We cleaned and polished each one before returning them to their owner.

Thought we would have another game yesterday afternoon and, as I did not like asking the Wing Commander for his clubs again, we went into a golf shop and hired a set for only three pence. A golf ball cost only sixpence, which was really cheap. Of course, it was less for us, as we were in uniform. St. Andrews is not a patch on Sandown or Shanklin for prettiness. Most of the houses are built of grey stone and look most depressing. There are very few flowers to be seen and I think that makes a place look more dull than it need do. The garden must be looking very good now, after you have done all that weeding. How are the onions, beetroot and other seeds that we planted coming along? Do not forget to put empty jars over the strawberries as it keeps the birds off and helps them to ripen. I will help you with some of the work when I come home next.

That seems so far away, my dearest wife.

All my love, Leslie

Monday June 16th 1941: A letter arrived from Monica which I answered at once. She kindly enclosed two VR badges, the darling. Went swimming and played billiards in the afternoon. There were extra signalling classes after tea.

> **Letter dated June 16th 1941** *from AC2 L. Harris at St Andrews.*
>
> *My sweet wife,*
>
> *Thank you for sending me the VR badges and the needle and thread, so that I can sew them on. If you get the chance can you get me a notebook? They seem in short supply here and I need it for my lecture notes. Thanks also for cleaning my bicycle for me. You seem to be doing all the jobs while I am away. Pleased to hear that Baby is putting on weight. He will look like a dumpling soon.*
>
> *With all my love and kisses.*
>
> *Your loving husband Leslie.*

Tuesday June 17th 1941: Got fatigues with Allen and George, for leaving our bedroom untidy.

Wednesday June 18th 1941: Maths exam. I do hope I get on alright. Went swimming in the afternoon for only a short time as the water was very cold. I spent the rest of the time writing letters.

Letter dated June 18th 1941 *from AC2 L. Harris at St Andrews.*

Monica love,

Received your letter dated the 15th this morning. Glad to hear from you for, my darling, your words are so cheering. They make me see you doing all the things you write about. Is it not lovely to think that, if all goes well, in about five more weeks I shall be home on leave. You are a dear to send me the chocolate and the book. I am always glad to get something to read before I turn in at night time. Tell Baby I will spank him if he is not a good boy always, but kiss him for me just the same. I went down to see the Pay Master today and have got the Southern Railway papers filled up, and are posting them off to the Station Master at Sandown, with your letter. Let me know if you do get any thing from them. Have you got your RAF pay through yet? I do hope so. Very little different has happened today. We have drill every day and, my goodness, do I sweat, but afterwards I feel fine. Last night I played billiards with my two pals for half an hour. It is sixpence a half hour at the Conservative Club. We might go again on Friday, but I have too much home work to do to go tonight.

I have seen that Pole I told you about a number of times since about the town. However, if I see him in the YMCA I shall be able to have another game of chess with him. The Poles are a funny lot for they salute each other and everyone else. They do not seem to bother what rank you are. Any amount of them salute us when we are out and it makes me feel a fool, returning it, when I am not yet an officer. They are very polite and courteous and nearly all of their officers say "Good Afternoon" when they are saluted, whether it is morning, afternoon or evening. There is a gas examination on Friday so I must swot up all my anti-gas notes. On the green, down by the seafront, is an old iron Russian gun. It must have been captured

during the Crimean War. How are the garden plants
growing? I wonder if there will be any fresh home-grown
peas by the time my leave is due? It has been hot today,
really too hot to be comfortable in uniform, but just the
sort of weather for a holiday. Was it not lucky we were
able to have our holiday together before I was called up. I
often think about it now and it is a comfort to think that
you are waiting at home for me. I feel down in the dumps
this evening and very homesick for you, so I have got all
your letters out and am reading them again, to cheer
myself up. Can you get my camera out and get Mother to
take some pictures of you and Baby and send them on to
me so that I can see you both again.

My dearest, I must get on with my swotting now.

With all my love to you my darling wife,

Leslie.

Thursday June 19th 1941: Started Navigation lessons, and was made a cadet subcaptain today. I had an interview with Pilot Officer Garcia, and found him OK.

Friday June 20th 1941: Gas exam this afternoon and I think I got on alright. I received a letter from Mother and a parcel from Monica, which had been sent on from Stratford. I have been issued with an aircraft identification book to study. Went with George to see a film called 'Torrid Zone'. It was quite good.

> **Letter dated June 20th 1941** *from AC2 L. Harris at St Andrews.*

> *Beloved,*

> *The parcel you sent to Stratford arrived here this morning.*
> *Thank you for enclosing my bathing costume. Now I shall*
> *be able to go swimming with the others in the evening.*
> *Yesterday I was made a cadet subcaptain. As you know,*

there are 50 fellows in our flight, and a chap named Wilson, who is 33 and was a schoolmaster before he joined up, is our cadet captain. There are 10 subcaptains and I am one of these. It is an unpaid job and is only a title and not a rank. It only lasts while we are here at ITW. A day or two ago I walked a little way out of St Andrews to a ruined castle and abbey. The castle was built on a very different plan to any other castle I have seen. In spite of the fact that it was in ruins, I doubt if it was built any earlier than the 17th century. I must try to get a book about it, or find someone who can tell me it's history.

As we went on parade this morning a Scottish Regiment marched past, together with their full band. All the bandsmen were in full Highland dress, but the rest were in battledress. They certainly were a grand sight. This morning we were interviewed privately by the CO. He is a new chap, but seems alright. He asked me if I liked St. Andrews so I told him that it was a very long way home. He put me down for the flight swimming team for there is to be an inter-squadron sports match soon. It is very quiet in the hotel now, for those who have not gone round to the YMCA are, as I am, writing letters and reading notes. I must close now, and go to the post office to catch the mail.

All my love, your loving husband, Leslie.

Saturday June 21st 1941: Had a haircut this morning. In the afternoon I was interviewed by Squadron Leader Bruce-Pearson. He seems very decent. In the evening I helped to take down tables at the Grand Hotel for a dance, but did not stay. I was going back at about eleven to replace the tables, but a violent storm began, so I went to bed instead. I sent Monica a fancy handkerchief, and to Mother, a needle case.

Sunday June 22nd 1941: Church parade in the morning and, in the afternoon, writing notes.

Monday June 23rd 1941: Lessons as usual and had a bathe in the afternoon. Hurrah! Two parcels from Monica.

Letter dated June 23rd 1941 **from AC2 L. Harris at St Andrews.**

My own dearest wife,

It is nearly ten at night and I am lying on my bed guzzling your cake, and the other good things your box contained. It is sweet of you to get such delicious stuff to eat, but you really must not spend what little money you have on things for me. I do hope your pay has arrived by now. We three, George, Allen and myself, have sampled your cake and are unanimous that it is a King of cakes. I am making it last as long as I can, but it is too nice to keep too long. The sergeant came in a few minutes ago, to see if we were all in bed, so I offered him a slice, which he accepted. He asked me who made it and I told him my wife. He said it was one of the best cakes he had ever eaten, so I gave him another slice. Many thanks for the exercise books you sent. They arrived just in time for we start an armaments course tomorrow, in place of the anti-gas course which has just ended. I will need the books for it. Love, if eggs are so scarce in Lake you must not make me those lovely tarts, but thanks for them, for they were the tops. Everything in the parcel was whole and unbroken, but there is a fair sized hole in the contents by now! Baby must be getting a big boy by now to have meat juice and rusks. Oh! How I wish I could see him and his little chubby face, the funny little man. Give him a kiss and a hug for me.

All my love, your loving husband, Leslie.

Tuesday June 24th 1941: Began armaments course today. Received a parcel from Mother and another letter from my dear wife. Answered the letter before going on guard. I am guard commander, with duty from 1900hrs to 0600hrs, but, of course, was not up all that time.

Letter dated June 24th 1941 from AC2 L. Harris at St Andrews.

My dear wife,

This letter may be a little dis-jointed, for it is 7.30 and I am in charge of the guard at this hotel. This sounds alright, but it means I have to be up most of the night to see that the other six take their turns of guard outside. Still, I am inside all night and have a bed by the desk, so I will be able to get some sleep. Just had to jump up and answer the telephone. Someone wants the sergeant so I have sent one of the guard off, to find him. I hope you do not have any more raids while I am away. Do you remember the bombs that came down at Lake, just after we were married? Did the bombs at Milton hurt any of your friends there? I hope not. It was indeed lucky that 25 Eastwood Road was not damaged. Allen, the fellow who comes from Gillingham, had a letter from home which says that Sittingbourne was badly damaged by hostile action. Please thank Mrs Jeffrey, in your next letter to her, for the socks she so kindly knitted for me. I doubt if she will be able to make me another pair, with wool now being rationed. We started a new course in armaments today and what little I learnt in the Home Guard about guns is going to be very useful indeed. There is a funny little army Padre about here and, every time we salute him, he always passes the time of day with us. On Sunday there was a Church Parade and I forgot to wear my uniform belt. Luckily, on inspection, the CO did not spot it. The service was given by the Chaplain General of the RAF. He talked about superstitions and, for once, I enjoyed listening to a service.

There was a brass tablet on the wall, near where I sat. It was in memory of an Able Seaman who lost his life on HM Submarine H3 in the Adriatic on the 16th of July 1916. This is the first of its kind I have yet seen.

Before going to bed yesterday my two pals and self forgot to book in. Luckily our own sergeant, Sgt Last, was on duty, and he marked us present. This morning he told us about it and said that if another sergeant on duty, who did not know us, he might have marked us absent. Then we would have been in trouble with the CO. Jolly good of him, was it not?

Darling, it is now 10.40, so you can tell how much I have been interrupted, so I must close down and post another guard. I have to do this at 12.10, 2,10 and 4.40 as well, and then I will try to get a little rest.

With all my love, sweet wife,

Your devoted husband, Leslie.

Wednesday June 25th 1941: Found lessons boring today so went to bed early.

Thursday June 26th 1941: Had a very busy day so, for a rest, George, Allen and myself went, in the evening, to the films. It was called 'The Farmer's Wife' and it was very good indeed.

Friday June 27th 1941: Received a parcel, containing strawberries, from Monica, also a letter from Mother and another from Marcus. In the evening I went round to the 60 Club for a game of billiards and to write up my notes on navigation.

Letter dated June 27th 1941 from AC2 L. Harris at St Andrews.

Monica my darling,

The strawberries you kindly sent to me arrived this morning, but they are eaten, every one, and jolly nice they tasted. They were a little over ripe, but nothing to trouble about. I am going to have my photograph taken tomorrow evening, for they take a week to get printed, and by then it will be pay day. I got a letter from Marcus today. I do not known when I will be able to reply for I have a great deal of notes to write up in my spare time. My cold is nearly better today, thank goodness, for it was a nuisance sneezing just as one of the lecturers came to an important part, and did they not give me a glare, because they had to repeat it again!

This afternoon we had a lecture on high altitude flying and I found it very interesting. There is to be a concert held here soon among us cadets and our officer has asked for volunteers to take part. Do you think they might like to hear me sing Waltzing Matilda?

Would you please look in my drawer and see if you can find my protractor and pair of compasses and send them on to me, please? They will be of great use in my navigation lectures.

I am glad to say I passed my anti-gas examination alright and, what is more important, the last maths exam. Only one person in 'B' flight failed, and he has been transferred over to become an Air Gunner, instead of an Observer. We are not told our individual marks but our flight Commander told us our average was 75% and over. He is quite pleased with us, for we are the top flight.

Today was the inter-squadron sports day and the CO said that he hoped that we would all go along to cheer on our squadron, so we thought we had better go. We all cheered

*very loudly but in spite of this, number 4 squadron was
last. Never mind, it was fun, and we all blamed our
sergeant far the lack of success, as, I believe I told you, his
name is Last! Quite by chance I met a fellow from 'C'
Flight today who as also named Harris and comes from a
village near Milton, I can not remember the name,
anyway, he has several relatives living in the
Sittingbourne area.*

*We three, George, Allen and myself, have found a quiet
cafe where you can buy a cup of tea and a cake for three
pence. We go there and take our lesson books with us and
do a lot of writing there. The people who run the place do
not mind and, as there is a radio, we can sometimes,
hear the news. I do miss not hearing the plays we used to
listen to at home.*

I must close now, beloved,

Your loving husband, Leslie.

Saturday June 28th 1941: In the afternoon the inter-squadron
sports were held. My squadron, No.4, came last; No.2 were first.
Parcels arrived from Monica. She is a dear for taking so much
trouble for my sake.

Sunday June 29th 1941: Church Parade in the morning. Wrote
letters home. Spent most of the spare time writing up my notes.
I had a round of putting with George and Allen.

Monday June 30th 1941: Lessons as usual. Went to extra
signalling lessons in the evening so had a round of putting before
going to bed. Received a letter from my sweet wife, which I
must answer tomorrow.

Tuesday July 1st 1941: Wrote to Monica and Mother today. I
was on fire picket so I could not go out.

Letter dated July 1st 1941 **from AC2 L. Harris at** St **Andrews.**

Sweet wife,

Thank goodness that I am not in charge of the guard every night. Only about once in ten days, like the Home Guard. I am glad your pay has come at last. How much is it? I should like to know as, for all the time I have been with the RAF, I have only been paid thirty shillings. I expect you will hear from the Railway soon now. Just like the Home Guard to keep you waiting for the money from them. It is just gone eight and I have done an hour's fire picket. I shall not be able to post this letter tonight as I am not supposed to go out and, anyway, the Post Office is shut. During dinner time I went for a short walk along the front with Wilson and, while we were down there, I saw a number of ducks and some baby ones, swimming in the sea. Wilson said they are called Diving Ducks, but he did not know their species. This is the first time I have ever seen ducks swimming in salt water.

I have just slipped down stairs with Allen for a cup of tea and some sardines as the cook has gone home. Both he and George and myself are on this fire picket duty together. I do hope you do not get any more raids while I am away. I do not like the idea of you being in danger and myself unable to be there to help you. You are lucky with the weather at home for here it has rained quite often during the last few days.

This is only a short letter because I have to get my uniform and boots cleaned before bed, as I shall not have time in the morning.

Good night and many kisses,

Your loving husband, Leslie.

Wednesday July 2nd 1941: Received another letter from Monica. It only left Sandown yesterday, so I answered it at once, Rain again during the day. After tea Allen and myself went to evening signalling classes.

Letter dated July 2nd 1941 from AC2 L. Harris at St Andrews.

Dear Monica,

Today lessons finished earlier than usual so I took a walk along the sand dunes before tea. I was thinking that in little more than two weeks I hope to start my leave. Then I shall be able to be with you and baby Noel again. In her last letter Mother said that when Baby has a rusk in his mouth he looked like Churchill smoking a big cigar. Do you think that is so? No, my dear, we have not had the swimming sports yet, when we hope to make up for our loss in the field sports. I have been in for a short dip this afternoon. We usually get a chance for a quick swim between lessons and it does help to freshen me up.

There is a shortage of writing paper at St Andrews and it has got so bad now that some of the fellows have used up all the toilet paper writing home so we now have to use newspaper. I have had to borrow this sheet from Allen to finish this letter.

On Monday the three of us went for a game of putting on the green. It is only one penny for a round of 18 holes so it is a cheap and jolly entertainment. George beat me by one stroke only and Allen was about six strokes behind. At tea someone knocked over a fire extinguisher and it went off. My hat, what a mess it made! One end of the room was all slippery with foam and all us cadets enjoyed it no end, but the Flight Sergeant nearly had a fit.

I cannot write any more now for I have run out of paper.

Bless you, beloved wife, Leslie.

Thursday July 3rd 1941: Went to the dentist in the afternoon and had two teeth filled. They did not hurt at all.

Friday July 4th 1941: Spent the evening from seven until nine at navigation classes.

Saturday July 5th 1941: Received a parcel from Monica, which cheered me up a lot. Spent the afternoon writing letters and notes. After tea I went to see the film "Hullabaloo".

*Letter dated July 5th 1941 **from AC2 L. Harris at** St **Andrews.***

Dearly beloved wife,

We heard last night that it was almost certain, if things continued as they are, we would all get leave in about two weeks. We were so overjoyed with the news that there was a pillow fight up and down stairs, with pillows, blankets and mattresses flying all over the place. The sergeant had to shout at the top of his voice to quieten things down, and that took a lot of doing. It was after eleven before we sorted out the blankets. Someone's pillow had broken a window but somehow the sergeant explained it away to the Officer, for nothing more has been said. I hope to leave here on Friday night the 19th July and get the night express from Edinburgh at 10pm. Then, if all goes well, should be home some time between 12 and 3pm on Saturday July 20th. I will find out the actual time later and will let you know when to expect me.

Many thanks for your last parcel, the cakes and pies were fine, and how did you manage to get all the sweets? I am so lucky to have married such a jolly good cook.

I have been able to find out a little about the local area. The Cathedral was built about 1160 by Bishop Arnold. During Edward the First's conquest of Scotland he stripped the roof of lead to make missiles for use against

Stirling castle. The Castle was built about 1200 by an English Bishop called Roger. It was later captured by the Scots and retaken by Edward I in 1298. It was lost to the Scots again and then won by the English in 1303. It was again in Scottish hands after Bannockburn but the English won it again in 1336.

So, my darling, there were many battles between the English and the Scots on these very fields which look so peaceful now. Nearly all of us are going to the concert that the RAF is giving. The tickets are one shilling each and we do not get them any cheaper than civilians, which is a swizz.

Well, I will close now by sending all my love.

Your ever loving husband, Leslie.

Sunday July 6th 1941: Church parade followed by an interview with the Squadron Leader during the morning. In the afternoon I wrote up my notes. I went to the RAF concert in the evening. Pilot Officer Garcia sang a comic song, it was very good.

Monday July 7th 1941: It is very hot today. I believe that I am improving in my signalling.

Letter dated July 7th 1941 from AC2 L. Harris at St Andrews.

Angel,

Your letter arrived this morning and I must answer it at once. For the last few days I have been writing up notes and swotting from seven in the evening until nearly midnight, as the examinations begin on Thursday week. We had a drill competition last Friday and our B Flight, which had practiced hard all week, came second out of the sixteen flights of numbers 1 to 4 Squadrons. The winners had all been in the RAF or army for over nine

*months. It has been a lovely warm day today so the
Sergeant said we could go to the swimming pool and take
a dip instead of drilling, as we were supposed to. The
water was very cold indeed, but I enjoyed it.*

*Have there been any raids lately? I should think that they
would have lessened now that Germany has to send so
many aircraft against Russia.*

*I must finish this letter now as I am so tired after all the
studying, and I can hardly keep my eyes open.*

All my love, Leslie.

Tuesday July 8th 1941: Working very hard at lessons and have very little time to spare. I do miss home a lot, still, it will not be long before I get leave. I had an interview with the Earl of Haddington this morning, but it was only a waste of time. Received letters from home today, how they cheer me up!

> ***Letter dated 8th July 1941*** *from AC2 L. Harris at St
> Andrews.*
>
> *My beloved wife,*
>
> *No sooner had I got back from the Post Office than I
> received your last letter. It has been nicely sunny today so
> I am sitting in my cubby hole on the beach writing to you.
> There is to be a swimming gala on Saturday afternoon
> and I am going in for the 100 yards breast stroke,
> 100yards backstroke, 200 yards freestyle, diving and
> walking the greasy pole, so you see I must put in a lot of
> practice.*
>
> *George cannot swim but he is going in for the greasy pole.
> Allen and myself have to stand by to pull him out every
> time he falls in. This is going to be a busy job!*

Allen is going in for the back and breast stroke. We do hope to win to make up for the loss in the athletics contest. I think we stand a good chance as there are a number of good swimmers in my flight. Our friendly rivals in A Flight are out to beat us, because we beat them in the drill competition.

George has to polish all the brass door knobs in the corridor because he went on parade without cleaning his buttons this morning, so Allen and myself are just going to help him.

Good night Angel, sweet dreams.

From your loving husband, Leslie.

Wednesday July 9th 1941: Very busy this morning, but we had the afternoon off for games. I went for a swim and then sunbathed until teatime.

*Letter dated July 9th 1941 **from AC2 L. Harris at St Andrews.***

Monica dear,

It has been another lovely day here today, but how hot it was in the lecture rooms. I have just been for tea, which was sausages, bread and jam. Tonight I am going down for a practice swim and then I will have to write up the day's lessons. George is just dressing to go on fire picket. It does seem silly to start at seven in the evening, but that is the rule. I am on guard duty tomorrow so I will not be able to write then, but I will again on Friday.

There is a rumour that we are to be issued with our flying kit tomorrow, but whether it is true or not I cannot say. The outfit costs over £60 alone, without the rest of our instruments, so we will have to be careful with them. I am

*sending a little gift for Noel, I hope he likes it. How is the
little fellow getting along? I am so looking forward to
seeing him, and you, when my leave begins.*

*By the way, did I tell you that, instead of motor taxis,
there are little horse drawn cabs here. We hope to get one
to take us to the station next week.*

My love to you both,

Your loving husband, Leslie.

Thursday July 10th 1941: Have very little spare time these
days as the exams begin on Monday. I was on guard duty again
this evening.

Friday July 11th 1941: We now have a piano, dart board, radio
and a table tennis table in the recreation room, so we did not go
out until just before ten. We went round to the YMCA for a cup
of tea and I had a short game of billiards with Allen, which I
won by a few points.

Saturday July 12th 1941: Squad drilling this morning. I had a
go at it myself. Two parcels from home came today. Oh, it is
nice to know that those at home are thinking of you.

*Letter dated July 12th 1941 **from AC2 L. Harris at** St
Andrews.*

My own sweet wife,

*Your parcels have arrived here safely today. Thank you so
very much for all the good things they contained. I took
some of the cakes down to the swimming pool this
afternoon, to eat after the races, for the swimming gala
was today. We went all out to win and just managed to
succeed by a few points. I was second in the backstroke
and third in the breaststroke, so I do not think that I did*

July 1941: "There is a rumour that we will be issued with our flying kit tomorrow. The outfit costs more than £60 alone."

too badly. I did not get a place in the diving, though Mr
Wilson, who is 31 and a former schoolmaster, who sleeps
in the next room to me, won it easily. The exams start
next week so, as today is the last holiday before them,
George, Allen and myself hope to be able to go to see a
gangster film at the cinema tonight. One thing not so
good is that when we leave St Andrews, Sergeant Last will
not be coming with us and the next NCO might not be
such a sport as he is. When I am on leave I am allowed
seventeen shillings and sixpence for food and am given
ration coupons. We will also take Baby for a walk out to
Alverstone to see Mr Plumbley. He may be able to let us
have some eggs. By the by, I have all the clothing coupons
from my old ration book, if they are any good to you. I
was talking to the cook a few days ago and told him
about the macaroni cheese that I made once. He thought
it was a good idea and, yesterday, he made some for tea,
but he used spaghetti instead!

So, my sweetest, I will close now,

Your loving husband, Leslie.

*Letter dated July 14th 1941 **from AC2 L. Harris at** St*
Andrews.

My darling wife,

Just a very quick note to let you know that I shall be
leaving here sometime on Friday afternoon. I hope to get
the 10pm train from Edinburgh and should arrive at
Sandown by 12.05 pm on Saturday. If I cannot catch the
night express I should be home about 2.06. We had our
group photograph taken this morning. I do not know if it
will be ready by Friday, but I hope so. The exams began

today and I have ,just taken the Morse sending test. I got
96% so I passed that alright. I am afraid I must close now
or else I might not catch the last post tonight.

All my love, your loving husband, Leslie.

Monday July 14th 1941: Wrote home to say I hoped to be home on Saturday. Passed the Morse buzzer sending test today with 96%.

Tuesday July 15th 1941: I got 100% in the Morse receiving test today! I have also passed the armaments examination.

Wednesday July 16th 1941: To relax from the exams I went to play cricket in the afternoon. Unfortunately I could not concentrate on the game and was easily caught.

Thursday July 17th 1941: I hardly got a wink of sleep last night through worrying about the remaining exams.

Friday July 18th 1941: Navigation examination, pay, dinner and then the 2.10 train for home, via Edinburgh, Berwick, Newcastle, York to London at 4.10. Taxi to Waterloo.

Saturday July 19th 1941: 5.27 from Waterloo with some RAF fellows from Blackpool. They are Air Mechanics. Three of them came on to the Island. Home with Monica and Baby at last. It rained in the afternoon, but went shopping with Monica. I bought a few stamps for my collection and then spent a quiet evening at home.

Sunday July 20th 1941: We went by train to Alverstone and, later, walked back. It was a very nice day.

Monday July 21st 1941: Went shopping in Sandown and bought some stamp mounts and spent most of the evening with my albums, and packing to go away on Friday.

Tuesday July 22nd 1941: Went with Monica and Baby to Shanklin. The day was lovely and we were very happy.

Wednesday July 23rd 1941: I bought same Kenya stamps yesterday, which I mounted in my albums, before packing them to go away. Spent some time with Mother before going to Shanklin to see Pickfords about moving the goods. Pickfords have nothing to pack the stuff in so it had better go by goods train.

Thursday July 24th 1941: The van called for the stuff, but, as it was not ready, they are going to call again tomorrow. Mother, sad at my going, said that St Nicholas, 19 Louis Road, Lake, will always be my home. She had my watch repaired and it came back today.

Friday July 25th 1941: Said cheerio to dear Mother this morning. Oh, please keep her safe until my next leave. The goods left early. There are 14 packages to go by goods train and two packages to go by passenger train. Monica, Baby and myself missed the train at Sandown so we went by taxi to Ryde and caught the boat in time. We had a good journey up to London and then on to Sittingbourne, having to change trains at Chatham. Baby was so good. I sent a letter to Mother to tell her of our safe arrival, and went to bed after supper.

Saturday July 26th 1941: It rained nearly all day today. I had my hair cut by a woman for the first time in a shop in Sittingbourne. Monica left Baby with a friend of hers so we were able to go to the Odeon where we saw a film called "The

Ghost of St. Michael's". It was jolly good indeed. Oh dear, I do not want to leave to go back to St Andrews, one little bit.

Sunday July 27th 1941: Kissed Monica Goodbye for the tine being, on Sittingbourne railway station at 7.27 this morning. I think she will be happy at Milton Regis until I get back on my next leave. Met George and his girl at Kings Cross and, shortly after, Allen came along. We met another fellow in our flight so us four were able to play cards during the journey. We passed York and Durham Cathedrals on the way North and saw the five Tyne bridges at Newcastle. By the time we got to Edinburgh most of the boys had joined the train. We had half an hour to spare on the station, so I had a cup of tea at the YMCA before going on to St Andrews.

Monday July 28th 1941: Very little to do as yet. Went for a bathe in the morning. The chaps who have failed in the exams were told so this afternoon. As I was not one of them, I believe I have passed. George failed in the navigation exam but he is likely to get another chance soon. I hope he passes then. Meteorology was the only lesson today. Wrote to Monica and Mother and then saw the film 'The Son of Monte Cristo' with Allen and George.

Tuesday July 29th 1941: Very little doing this morning, but lessons, as usual, in the afternoon. Wrote to Monica and Mother in the evening. Had a few games of table tennis and billiards with the boys, until it was time for bed.

Wednesday July 30th 1941: Lessons in the morning, but after lunch it was games time. George, Geoffrey and myself played golf. I won one game and Geoffrey the other. Allen did not come as he was writing letters. Poor George cannot go to the lessons any more, as he is to remuster as a Wireless Operator/ Air Gunner.

Thursday July 31st 1941: Received a letter from Mother today, enclosing a snap of herself. I am glad to hear from home and the photo is very good. I wonder when I shall hear from my wife? I hope she is settling down in Sittingbourne and is liking it. I was inoculated again today, for the fourth time. It is the last dose, we all hope, for some time to come. George is too tall to be a Wireless Operator/Air Gunner so he is remustering as a ground wireless operator. Good luck to him.

Friday August 1st 1941: Pay day today, but I intend to try to save ten shillings to buy a book on Air Navigation. Received a very nice letter from Monica today and I wrote an answer to her and also to Mother. I played a round of putting with George in the evening. The Wing Commander inspected our rooms today and did not think much of them. In fact we are likely to get extra drill tomorrow. George is to move down into the Grand Hotel tomorrow as he joins D Flight. This is a great pity for we have been together for nine weeks.

Saturday August 2nd 1941: Room 45 is one of the lucky rooms for we are not on extra drill this afternoon, like most of the flight.

Sunday August 3rd 1941: Church parade this morning then spent most of the afternoon sleeping and writing notes. On guard duty from 01.38hrs to 03.48hrs on Monday morning.

Monday August 4th 1941: Received parcels from both Mother and Monica today. Went for a short route march in the afternoon, followed by Navigation until 1800hrs. The trouble now at Navigation lessons is that the master admits that they have not the proper equipment to teach us with. Feel a bit homesick today and will be glad to get some more leave. Bought four aircraft identification books for eight shillings. I also got a letter from Edgar Allen.

Tuesday August 5th 1941: The same as any other day, so have little to note, except that Allen and myself went round to the 60 Club for a cup of tea and a game of billiards before turning in for the night. I received a parcel from Mother containing some paper paste and a book. As the paste was all I wanted I began to make an aircraft identification book of every aircraft that I can find anything about.

Wednesday August 6th 1941: Lessons in the morning but after lunch some of us went down for a game of cricket. It was A and B Flights versus C and D Flights. The latter won by two runs only.

Thursday August 7th 1941: Drill, Physical Training and Navigation took up this morning while, after lunch, two hours were spent in private study and the remaining time at signalling and armaments. Have not received a letter from Monica since Monday. I do hope I get one tomorrow as I like to hear a lot from her.

Friday August 8th 1941: received a parcel from Monica this morning, containing lovely cakes and things. I am thankful to hear from her as the last letter was on Monday. I saw the film 'Scarface' in the evening.

Saturday August 9th 1941: Lessons during the morning but, after lunch, we were free. After tea Allen and myself went to see the film 'Spare a Copper', it was very good. Went out on manoeuvres at 11.30pm.

Sunday August 10th 1941: I was out with the Home Guard guarding a hut until after twelve noon, but nothing happened. We were given some fireworks which we set off at the Imperial. Slept for most of the afternoon but wrote to Monica and to Mr Attrill at Sandown station about Monica's allowance.

Monday August 11th 1941: Went to bed. early to make up for the sleep I lost on Saturday night. Received a parcel from Monica and two parcels and a letter from Mother, which I answered at once.

Tuesday August 12th 1941: Spent the evening writing up my notes. We had one of our lessons in a film this morning.

Wednesday August 13th 1941: As it began to rain Allen and myself went to the films during the afternoon to see a film called 'Blond Inspiration'. It was poor.

Thursday August 14th 1941: Lessons as usual, but after tea, Allen, Gibbs and myself went to the films to see 'Angel over Broadway'. It was a very good film and I enjoyed it very much. As we were nearly broke, we had to go in the eight pence seats.

Friday August 15th 1941: Received a parcel from Monica, containing all manner of good things, this morning. She is sweet to take so much trouble on my behalf. My pay was three pounds ten shillings today, instead of one pound, as it usually is. I do not know yet why the increase but I banked two pounds in the Post Office. Went out for a game of putting, after tea, with Allen.

Saturday August 16th 1941: This morning I received a letter from Monica telling me of home news. The sports were to take place this afternoon but it rained so hard that they had to be cancelled. Instead I went with Ewart and Hayden to the films to see 'The Trial of Mary Doogan'. It was quite good. I spent the evening with my aircraft recognition books. Yesterday I bought two nine shilling and sixpence books second-hand for twelve and six.

Sunday August 17th 1941: Church parade this morning. Before lunch I wrote to Monica in answer to her letter of yesterday. I went to the sports in the afternoon. My squadron lost again. Went to the evening service with Allen. Ewart and Allen Vaughn were an fire picket. When we came out of church we went to the RAF concert, which was very good indeed. It was late in ending and I did not get to bed until about a quarter to eleven. Allen was already asleep.

Monday August 18th 1941: Received a roll of film and a letter today, from Monica. It was good of her to get it for me. After tea I went to the cinema with Short and another fellow from his room as Allen is saving up to get married, and will not spend any money these days. The film was called 'Sky Devils', but it was not very good. I went round to the YMCA with Allen, for a cup of tea, before bed. I cut my hand on a shell while on the beach during PT, quite painful.

Tuesday August 19th 1941: Two parcels from Mother, how jolly decent of her to send me the papers and chocolate. The others went for a swim this morning. I could not because of the cut on my hand. Instead I took a photo of some of the lads in their swimming costumes and also a snap of the Sergeant. After tea I played a game of billiards with Allen against Allison and Oramshire. They won easily. Later wrote to mother and my dear wife in reply to their last letters. I then went to the YMCA for our usual cup of tea before bed, and met Sparks with his 'sister'. At least, that is what he told us, but I very much doubt it! We received our Leading Aircraftman badges this afternoon and spent most of the afternoon sewing them on our uniforms.

Wednesday August 20th 1941: Navigation, armaments and signals were the lessons for this morning. It should have been sports in the afternoon but, as it began to rain very hard, Allen and myself went to the films to see 'Inspector Hornleigh Goes To It' and 'The Return of the Cisco Kid'. Both were very good. After tea four of us went to the All Saints Club in North Castle

Street, for a game of billiards. Allen and myself played as partners and just lost by a very small margin.

Thursday August 21st 1941: Received a parcel from Monica this evening but, as I was on fire picket, I have not been able to answer it. Must do so without fail tomorrow. Jolly nice parcel.

Friday August 22nd 1941: B Flight won the squadron drill competition and, as a prize, are going to Leauchars tomorrow afternoon. After tea, as Allen was writing, I went to the films myself, to see 'This England'. It was an excellent picture. I met Allen after the show and we played billiards at the All Saints Club until ten.

Saturday August 23rd 1941: I sprained my ankle playing football in the morning and as a result was unable to go to the aerodrome. I was sorry at missing this but the boys were jolly good and told me all about it when they came back.

Sunday August 24th 1941: My right ankle is much better so went on Church parade, as usual, this morning. Spent the rest of the morning writing home, and to Mr Attrill at Sandown station to tell him about my promotion so to arrange the pay I get from the railway. After lunch Allen and myself went out for a walk and met George and Carrow at the Steep Rock so we four sat talking until after four. George went to the Grand for his tea while the three of us came back for our own.

As tea was late I took three photos of ourselves in our flying kit, until the meal was ready. I had also taken three other pictures down at the Steep Rock. After tea, as Allen was on fire picket, Carrow and myself went out for a walk. We met Allen on the way and the three of us went into the old churchyard by the ruins of the Cathedral where we discovered an old crypt. We went a little way in but, as it was very dark, and seemed half full of water, we did not go in far, and came out quickly. We went round by the harbour and out on to the jetty before calling in at the YMCA for a cup of tea. We heard the Prime Minister speaking on the wireless, before returning to bed.

Monday August 25th 1941: I sent Monica a present of a pendant because of the 27th August. In the evening I went to see a film called 'The Saints Vacation'. It was quite good. We all went on a route march from 10.30 until 4.30.

Tuesday August 26th 1941: An easy day today. I wrote letters home and then went to bed early.

Wednesday August 27th 1941: On this day two years ago I met my wife-to-be at Shanklin. I was on guard duty from 9.30 until 12 midnight. All quiet.

Thursday August 28th 1941: I received a parcel from Mother, which was jolly decent of her. There was an R.A. test in the afternoon. It was a farce. Saw a film called 'Dr Kildare's Crisis', it was not too bad.

Friday August 29th 1941: A parcel of cakes, and other nice things, arrived from Monica. In the evening I went to the 60 Club for supper.

Saturday August 30th 1941: Went with Allen, as usual, to the pictures. The film was called 'No No Nanette'. It was very good, but on the farcical side. In the afternoon we went to Leauchars and looked over several aircraft types such as the Wellington, Beaufort, Hudson, Lockheed Transport, Magister, Tiger Moth, D.H. Air Liner, Gladiator and Lysander. It was Queen Wilhelmina's birthday and all the Dutch pilots were on leave. All those aircraft and no flight!

Sunday August 31st 1941: Church parade in our ceremonial belts. Had an easy afternoon writing up notes. I went to the church of Scotland with about six of the boys, and stayed for tea afterwards.

Monday September 1st 1941: Had a letter from Monica to say that Figgaro had three kittens last Monday. Went to see 'Arise My Love' after tea, and it was very good. It began at the end of the Spanish Civil War and went all through the Second Great War, up to the surrender of France. The sinking of the *Athenia* was very well done.

Tuesday September 2nd 1941: I had a letter from Monica this morning, which I answered and sent her some chocolates as well. I also wrote to Mother.

Wednesday September 3rd 1941: Lovely warm day so I went with the boys for a swim, but the water was very cold. In the evening Allen, Stan and myself went to see 'Ride Kelly Ride' at the New Picture House. It was not too bad. Our posting came through and we believe it is overseas. Hope to go on leave on Monday, for a week.

Thursday September 4th 1941: Kit inspection during the morning.

Friday September 5th 1941: We were issued with tropical kit, or at least, part of what we are to get. I passed the Medical Officers inspection during the morning. We were told, late in the evening, that we were to go on leave tomorrow morning, so had to hurry up to get packed.

Saturday September 6th 1941: Newcastle. A very rushed morning getting ready to leave. As the passes were late in coming through I nearly missed the train from St Andrews but the CO went down in his car to fetch them, so we all just managed to get down to the station in time. There was a wait at Edinburgh which enabled me to get tea at the YMCA and to walk down Princes Street. Arrived at Newcastle at 08.30pm and had to wait until 10.45 for the London train. I went to sleep as soon as I was inside.

Sunday September 7th 1941: London – Sittingbourne. Arrived at Kings Cross about six, and travelled to Waterloo Junction by Underground train. I was lucky to catch a train at once for Sittingbourne, but it was a slow, stopping one and I had to change at Chatham. Dearest Monica and baby Noel were waiting on the station for me though I had been unable to let her know when I should arrive. As I walked to Milton Regis with my sweet wife I was so very happy, but Monica was a little sad when I told her that this was my embarkation leave. She soon had an excellent breakfast ready for me, which I made short work of, as I was very hungry.

After lunch we took a walk to a place called the Grove, which is a pretty park like place by a cricket ground. We bought some ice cream, and Baby enjoyed the pieces which Monica gave him. Looked through my postage stamp albums during the evening, and mounted one or two stamps which I had acquired during the past six weeks. Went to bed just after ten after a very happy day.

Monday September 8th 1941: Milton Regis. We went shopping in Sittingbourne, where I bought some stamps for my collection. Later we walked to a little village called Borden. It was a very nice walk, and we saw lots of ripe Victoria plums on the trees. Monica had some Victoria's at home, which we ate when we got back, and very nice they were too! Called in the evening to see if a friend of Monica's would look after baby tomorrow whilst we went to Canterbury.

Tuesday September 9th 1941: Canterbury. Monica and myself went by an early train to Canterbury, after leaving Baby with Mrs Beech. I enjoyed the journey very much and we changed trains at Faversham where Monica said an Aunt of hers lived. We had lunch as soon as we arrived and, afterwards, went shopping. We bought a fluffy dog for Noel and Monica tried to get a pocketbook to hold my stamps while I am travelling, but the shop was out of stock. I bought a number of stamps at the same time. Next we walked in the Dane John Gardens, which is a small park near to the station. To my surprise I saw a very large howitzer in position and men building more gun emplacements; also there is a great deal of barbed wire and other defence posts.

We went into the museum, which I enjoyed a great deal, then we had a sardine salad tea followed by strawberry ice cream. We took another look around the city before taking the train for home. We collected Baby from Mrs Beech and turned in after an enjoyable day.

Wednesday September 10th 1941: London. Up early this morning as I was going down to see Mother. Monica was up to see me off so I kissed her and hurried to catch the train. Change at Chatham and London Bridge, but found that the train from Waterloo had no connection with the Isle of Wight boat so waited until the 10.15am train. I spent the time by sending a telegram to Mother saying that I would be home on the 2.6 train. Then I walked along the Embankment to see Cleopatra's Needle and other monuments, after crossing the Thames by a bridge. Walking along I passed Scott's vessel *Discovery* and crossed back to the South bank over Waterloo bridge.

Very little air raid damage to be seen in some parts of London, while others are very badly destroyed. Going over on the boat I felt so happy as the Island came nearer and nearer. I met one of my old railway friends on Ryde Pier Head. He had been the Guard of the train that hit the crossing gates at Alverstone. He said he hoped I was getting on well, and enjoyed RAF life. I didn't tell him that I did as well as I do. Mother was on the platform at Sandown to meet me and I was overjoyed to see her again. At home, a delicious dinner awaited us. After washing up and playing with Figgaro, who does not miss her three kittens, who have new homes now, we walked to Shanklin down Green Lane. We had tea with Aunt Rose before going to the Regal to see a film called 'The Prime Minister'. It was very good indeed. We went back to see Eileen and Aunty Edie before returning home. Had supper, and then, went to bed. It was fine to be in my own bed, in my own room, once more. I wish this silly war would end, and we could all settle down happily on the Island again. Earlier we found that Mother had left her handbag, containing the door keys, at Shanklin. I had to climb in by the kitchen window to open the front door!

Thursday September 11th 1941: Lake, Isle of Wight. Up at seven and, after breakfast, we walked to the railway station. As we were early I looked in to see Mr Attrill. I was sad at saying cheerio to Mother, but do hope to be back again with her soon. I had hoped to meet Monica at Victoria but as she was not there I went to the News Cinema until the Sittingbourne train was due. When I arrived back Monica told me that she had been unable to go up to London as Mrs Beech was out, and so there was no one to look after Baby. We then had a late lunch before going shopping. This is the anniversary of our wedding day, and all I can say is that I have been very happy all the time, except when I have been away.

Friday September 12th 1941: Faversham. Today Monica and myself went by bus to Faversham. We had intended to go by train, but we left it a bit late so, rather than hurry, we took the bus. It was a very nice journey and, when we got out at our destination, we took a look around the town. In one shop Monica brought me a chessboard and ordered a Stamp Collector's Wallet, as a gift, for yesterday we had been wed just one year. I bought one or two stamps for my collection and a book to read on my journey on Monday. Next we looked over the church but, as it is fairly new, I did not find much of interest, except one or two pieces of old brass. It has an unusual open-work type of spire on a square topped tower. This is the first of this type that I have seen. We then went to tea with Monica's Aunt, who is quite a nice old lady. She made a great fuss of baby Noel. Her adopted daughter was also there for tea. After the meal we said goodbye and took a bus back to Sittingbourne. Mother sent us a nice fruit set as a wedding anniversary gift. I am paying for Monica to have a radio-relay fixed up, as my present to her, as she said that she would like it.

Saturday September 13th 1941: Milton Regis. Wrote to Mother thanking her for yesterday's gift. I took Noel shopping in the afternoon, while Monica was kindly baking cakes and other nice things for me. After tea Monica and myself left Baby with Mrs Goldfinch when we went to see the film called 'Pimpernel Smith'. It was very good. There was a short air raid warning, but it did not last long.

Sunday September 14th 1941: Milton Regis. I went round to the station in the morning to find out when the trains left tomorrow for St Andrews. I was told that the timetables were locked up, so I must go back later. After dinner Monica put Noel in his pram and we went again to the railway station. We then took a last walk round the orchards, but it began to rain so we returned for tea. Together we had a happy evening but packing was not so cheerful. I have been so very happy this week, and do not like to leave tomorrow.

Monday September 15th 1941: Up early and breakfasted before going to the railway station. As it was too early for Noel to be out, I kissed him in his cradle and picked him up to tell him to be a good boy until I come back. It was so difficult to kiss Monica, and to know that it would be some little time before I shall see her again. Like the brave darling she is she did not cry until the train drew out of the station, and hands that held until this last moment parted. Then I saw tears fall from her lovely eyes. Oh God, keep her safe and protect her until I return. We waved until the train turned a corner and we could no longer see each other.

The journey to Edinburgh was uneventful, but, at Newcastle, I saw quite a lot of air raid damage. One crater was practically on the rail road, and workmen were repairing the signal wires. Just outside Newcastle I saw a second church with an open-work steeple, but, unlike the one at Faversham, it was dirty and ugly.

I met MacKinnley and Palmer on the train to St Andrews. Of course, all the rest of the boys were there when we arrived at the Imperial. I was surprised when I learnt that Allen, and some twenty of B Flight, had left, without any leave, for Canada. Allen left my snaps with the Sergeant, so I will send them home tomorrow. Tonight I just unpacked my kit and turned in to bed.

Tuesday Sept 16th 1941: St Andrews. Wrote home to Monica and Mother and got a parcel from Mother and a letter from my wife, which had been waiting since I left on leave. Very little to do today so I went, with Carr to see the film 'Target for Tonight'. It was a fair film, but not too good for the type it should be.

Wednesday September 17th 1941: Forth Bridge. After the lorry had taken our kit away we played cards until teatime. I sent a gift of a handkerchief case each to Monica and Mother, as a farewell gift. I hope they like them. The CO wished us Good Luck before we left, and came down to the station and shook us by the hand before we left.

The Earl of Haddington inspected us before we marched down to the train. Allen must be well away on the high seas by now, so it is doubtful that I will catch up with him in England. All that is left of the old B Flight came to see us off, and I do hope we all meet again one day.

We changed trains at Leuchars and Edinburgh. As the train crossed over the Forth Bridge for the sixth time I tossed a penny into the water for Good Luck. After passing Carlisle I went to sleep.

Thursday September 18th 1941: Wigan. Awoke at 5.30am at Wigan, where I had a cup of tea. Played cards in the train for the rest of the journey. Went via St Helens, arriving at Liverpool Lime Street about 7.40am. It was funny, being back at the city where I was born. We marched from Lime Street to the Underground station. Saw St George's Hall and Wellington's Column. I also saw a tram going to West Kirby, where I was born. We went by train to West Kirby, on the River Dee, and from there, to the depot by motor lorry. There we reported, and were shown to our sleeping room which holds about twenty fellows. We had an early tea or rather, dinner, as we had missed breakfast. Tea was at 4.30pm and Supper at 7.30pm. The meals are good, but not so nice as home fare. There are only eight, including myself, of the old B Flight here. I wrote to Monica and Mother to tell them that I was alright and that I hoped that they were.

Friday September 19th 1941: West Kirby. Up at 6.30am and, after breakfast, waited an hour or so for a very quick MO inspection. Then, during the afternoon, we were issued with most of our tropical kit. The rest of the time we spent reading. In the evening four of us took a walk to West Kirby, a distance of about two miles. We bought a cup each to drink our tea from, as we had not yet been issued with any yet. I sent a picture post card each to Mother and Monica, before going to the films to see 'City for Conquest'. It was fair. I walked back in the half light and thought of home.

Saturday September 20th 1941: Liverpool. Spent the morning in camp but, at four, I managed to get an Out of Bounds pass, so I went over to Liverpool. After a journey by train and bus, I arrived at last in Utting Avenue. The waste land where the old stream ran has now been turned in to a very nice park, and all the empty ground has been built upon, except the corner at Queen's Drive, which is as it was eleven years ago.

As I passed 254, my old home, I asked a newspaper boy if Mrs Perry still lived in this road. He told me the number of her house was 246. Phil opened the door, and I recognised him at once. He remembered me, and my goat, as soon as I introduced myself. His mother was glad to see me, and made me quite at home. Jack came in, and he is a very fine lad of thirteen. When last I saw him he was just crawling. Mrs Perry gave me tea, which was very good of her. She went round to fetch her friend Mrs Donalson and her son Adrian. Adrian knew me at once. They stayed, talking for a long time, before leaving. Jack is very interested in aeroplanes and has a number of very good models. Phil had to leave about seven, as he is on night work at the docks.

Mrs Perry asked for Mother's address, so that she can write to her. I stayed until half past nine, then I said Cheerio and Jack took me up to the tram stop at Cherry Lane. I found that I had forgotten my gas mask, so he went back for it. A 43 tram came along, so I said good night and returned to the city. I managed to catch the 10.20 pm train to West Kirby and walked back to camp.

Sunday September 21st 1941: West Kirby. Church parade at West Kirby this morning, which meant a walk of over two miles each way, and it was dinner time before we got back. I did not go out until 3pm and then I only walked in to West Kirby to send a postcard to Monica and Mother, giving them my new address. Spent the rest of the evening playing cards.

Monday September 22nd 1941: Hoylake. Very dull day indeed, but I wrote letters home, and read. After tea three of us walked into Hoylake, which is about one and a half miles over the fields. We intended to go to the films, but, as we had seen the one there, we took a bus to West Kirby. Before we went to the cinema I posted my letters and registered one for Monica as there were two pounds inside to help pay for a cot for Noel. We saw the film 'Kipps' by H.G. Wells, and it was very good indeed. On the way back we bought some fish and chips which we ate walking back to camp.

Tuesday September 23rd 1941: Meols. Spent the morning reading. We had lunch early because we had to parade at 12.45hrs. There must have been over one thousand men, but only a small proportion were aircrew. We marched to Hoylake through Meols, and went to the cinema where we saw 'Pygmalion' and 'Target for Tonight'. They were both good, but I saw the latter in St Andrews. We did not march back, so four of us went by train back to West Kirby, where we had tea. I bought a bottle of powder to send back to Monica before we returned to camp.

Wednesday September 24th 1941: West Kirby Camp. Very dull day, in the morning I went to the tailors and got them to sew my badges on my tropical uniform. I received a letter from Mother, which had been re-addressed from St. Andrews. I wrote back to her and also to Monica. I went on guard duty at four in the afternoon. When I came off my turn of duty I found a nice long letter from Monica waiting for me. This was about 2am Thursday morning. Jim and George were on duty with me and we livened things up by stopping everyone for their identity cards. I have put in for a pass to go over to Liverpool again tomorrow.

Thursday September 25th 1941: West Kirby. I could not get my pass today because I was told that we might leave at any time now. All those from St Andrews are in 423 draft and we had to print RORO/D on our kit bags. This is a code to show our destination. I received a letter from Mother this morning so I spent the afternoon writing home. We are not allowed out of camp after 5pm, but I managed to get past the guard and walk into West Kirby. It was a very clear day and I got a good view over the river Dee into the hills of Wales. In the town, I called first at the Post Office to send the jar of powder to Monica and a little money gift to Mother to pay for the radio licence. I bought two books to read on the voyage and was lucky to get a lift back to camp in a lorry returning from the railway station.

Friday September 26th 1941: Birkenhead. I managed to get a day pass for Liverpool so I left camp a little after nine in the morning. I went by two buses to the landing stage at Birkenhead, and crossed the Mersey by ferry. I was excited by the sight of the Liver Building on the other side. I went by number 43 tram to Utting Avenue. I walked to the cemetery and, after ascertaining from the office that the number of my Father's grave was 18-411, I walked to it. I only stayed a short time, thinking of so many happy times the three of us had enjoyed in days gone by. I enquired at a mason's outside the gates if they would clean the grave up a little, but they were so vague that, in the end, I had to leave it.

I bought two buns and a meat pie, which I ate in the little park close by to my old home. This I did because it was lunch time and I did not want to put Mrs Perry to the trouble of giving me dinner. Then I called on her, and found that both she and Jack were in, but Phil was at work. Jack left at one to go back to school, so Mrs Perry took me out and introduced me to Miss Law. She is Sydney's elder sister who was old when I was small. She seemed pleased to see me, and asked how Mother was. Then we went to pay a call on Mrs Williams, but she was out. Mrs Williams has married again, but Mrs Perry does not remember her second name.

We then went back to 246 Utting Avenue. Jack was home and took me for a short cycle ride, to show me some of the air-raid damage done locally. It is very extensive in many places. After tea, I stayed until half past nine, at which time I left on my return journey. I was sorry to have missed Phil, but I may get a chance of seeing him again before we leave. I went by rail from St James street, to Meols and walked the rest of the way back to camp. There were letters from Monica and Mother waiting for me. In Monica's there was a nice diary for next year. She also writes to say that she has already sent off my pocket stamp wallet, which she is giving me as a gift as we have been married a whole year. I will go up to the mail office first thing tomorrow to see if it is there.

Saturday September 27th 1941: Birkenhead. Monica's gift was waiting in the office, and it is a lovely book, just the very thing I required to hold postage stamps while travelling. I wrote at once, thanking her for being the darling she is. I am so glad that I married her, for she is a very good wife and I love her so much. I wrote home to Mother, as well, to tell her that, as yet, I have not received the last parcel which she sent to St Andrews.

In the afternoon George, Ken and myself tried to get a bus to Chester, but, as it was full, we were unable to go. Instead we went by train to Birkenhead, where we had tea at a little shop. Afterwards we saw a film called 'Andy Hardy's Private Secretary'. It was not too bad, on the whole. After the show we went back by railway train.

Birkenhead is badly damaged in many parts, but nothing of importance seems to be hit. Of course, I have not seen the docks, which, I believe, are also damaged. Birkenhead is out of bounds without a pass, and, as we did not have one, we were lucky not to be pulled up. On getting back to camp, after buying fish and chips in West Kirby, I found a telegram waiting for me. It was from Monica asking me if she should come up to West

Kirby. This was sweet of her but, because of the distance, and baby Noel, I was obliged to send a reply saying that, though I wanted to see her with all my heart, it was not really worth it.

Sunday September 28th 1941: West Kirby Camp. We leave here tomorrow, so we were unable to go out of camp, and I am glad I told Monica not to come up. Our kit bags left during the afternoon. I wrote letters home, these I expect will be the last I will be able to send before we sail. Oh God bless and protect all my dears during the coming winter, and for ever.

My Journeys on the Dark Continent at the time of the Second Great War

H.M. Troopship *Duchess of Richmond* left Liverpool and Mersey River on the last day of September 1941 and on the 14th of October of the same year, dropped anchor in the harbour of Freetown, Sierra Leone. Southwards we sailed until we rounded the Cape of Good Hope and by November the 3rd we were at Durban. My journey from here was by rail across Natal to Lyttelton Camp in Transvaal. It was during my stay here that I visited Pretoria and Johannesburg. On the 18th of December we were entrained for No.45 Air School at Oudtshoorn, Cape Province, where we arrived two days later. While at Oudtshoorn I spent a number of happy days at Mossel Bay, a small seaside town some 56 miles away over the Actaquas Mountains.

My fate decreed that, for fifteen weeks, I should continue my training as an Aerial Navigator, which included everything except flying the blasted aircraft! For over three months I lived to the monotonous drone of aero engines, to navigate in Ansons and to bomb with Oxfords. I flew all over the mountains of the Cape and out over the Indian Ocean – to some people, flying like a glorious bird, but to those who flew in them, The Devils Own Invention!

Monday September 29th 1941: Liverpool Docks. We paraded in full kit at 08.15 this morning and, after being issued with rations, we left about nine for West Kirby. From there we travelled by train to Liverpool. Here we changed to a bus which took us on to the quay where our ship lay. We all embarked at 11.00 hrs and I had a nice bunk on the promenade deck. There are a large number of troops on board, but they are on decks below us and are very tightly packed. They are not so well off as we cadets are. I watched the holds being loaded with all sorts of gear and kit. A sailor was packing tins, like large meat containers, into watertight boxes in the lifeboats, so I asked him what they contained. He told me it was chocolate, in case we had to take to the boats. From the top, or sun-deck, I could see the immense damage done to the dock buildings round about. The loss of life and goods must have been very heavy. The ship appears to carry no fixed guns of any description, but two mobile light AA guns are mounted on the top deck. At 5.15pm or thereabouts, the ship was towed by tugs in to a new basin, nearer the river. Tea was just after six, and it was most enjoyable. We are to sleep in our clothes until we are out of the danger area.

Tuesday September 30th 1941: Mersey River. I was up a little after six this morning, and after washing and polishing my buttons, I went up on deck. During the night we had moved up to another quay. From the boat-deck I had a good view of Liverpool and the other side of the river. Ships of the convoy were already assembling outside in the river. At 07.45hrs I went below for breakfast and, while I was eating, the ship was moved, by two tugs named *Nelson* and *Wellington*, out into the river. From the ship I could make out the Liver Buildings over the tops of the docks. We had lifeboat drill during the morning, and have been told always to carry our lifejackets while the ship is in the danger area. About 1500hrs our ship began to move out into open water. We seem to be in the van of the convoy, for other ships followed us. We passed two sunken ships, marked by wreck buoys, in the fairway. On the ship sailed, passing no less than four more wrecks, at long intervals, grounded near to the Lancashire shore. I could see Blackpool Tower from my seat on the deck rails. From the other side I could see the hills of Wales rising away into the distance. As the ship sailed over the bar I went below decks as I was getting a little cold. I took out my photographs, and looked at them a long time, thinking of home and all I love. Oh God, keep us all safe during this hellish war! After tea I read, and mended a seam in my jacket which had come unsewn. Today I noted that the ship has a small fixed gun on the poop deck, and four machine guns on the sun-deck.

Cigarettes are only one shilling and three pence for 50, so the chaps that smoke are very pleased. I had a lot of ginger marmalade for tea, which was jolly good. Just took a walk round the deck, before turning in for the night. As the sun set I saw we were sailing just a few points North of West. A destroyer has come up in front of the ship and both have been signalling to each other by Aldis lamp. The two aeroplanes that have been with us during the afternoon have now left.

Wednesday October 1st 1941: At sea. Up at 05.40hrs, sea quite rough, there is land on both sides, must be islands. Some of the boys were not down to breakfast, so I got two helpings of sausages. Boat drill this morning, many chaps seasick. Only seven out of eighteen down for dinner, and eight for tea. Feeling none too good myself, so will write no more tonight.

Thursday October 2nd 1941: Off Iceland. More than 75% of personnel seasick, so very few down in mess. I have not yet been seasick, which is a wonder, as I have been drinking fizzy lemonade. The convoy has 27 merchantmen, 2 cruisers, 7 destroyers and an aircraft carrier that looks like the *Argus*. The leading cruiser is of the County class and one of the destroyers is one of the ex USA flush-deckers. There have been three 'Action Stations' warnings during the day, but they came to nothing. Passed Iceland early this morning, but I do not know where we are now.

Friday October 3rd 1941: At sea. It was quite dark when I got up this morning and, as it was a little after six, we must be moving West. A soldier died last night and was buried at sea this morning. I did not hear of any service being held, but the flag flew at half mast. He had only just come out of hospital, and was not fit to travel so far. The weather is much better, and I sat on the forecastle, reading, this morning. Then the destroyer on the far port side opened fire on an aeroplane, which I just saw, before diving for cover. The Warning signal lasted for over two hours, but nothing else took place. When I came on deck after the 'All Clear', I saw we were in a heavy mist, and could only just see the boats on either side. About a dozen small birds were flying low over the water, close to us, on the port side. After lunch, which I enjoyed, I saw that a ship next to us was towing two large painted boards. I was told that this was to enable the following ship to keep in line during mist or at night. Aircraft from the carrier were on patrol throughout the day. Made a very good meal of fried herrings, bread and jam, for tea. Later I took a walk round the deck, and was amazed to see a number of flying fish leaping out of the water. I thought that we were too far North for them, but a fellow said that, now and again, they were to be seen in the North Atlantic.

Saturday October 4th 1941: North Atlantic Ocean. The convoy broke in two this morning. About seven merchantmen, one of the cruisers, and at least two destroyers stayed on the Westerly course, bound, no doubt, for America, while we turned towards the South. A very nice afternoon, though it rained early in the day. What I took yesterday to be flying fish might have been the white underbodies of small birds, which are often flying near the ship. The blackout was not over until 09.11hrs this morning. I trust to God that all at home are well and happy. Baby Noel will be quite big when I see him in six or seven months, if all goes well. I had a hot seawater bath tonight, with some special soap I got from the canteen. Jim Branyer and myself were first up this morning, so we had an early morning cup of tea from the canteen. I noticed that there are two Lewis guns and two Bren guns mounted on the bridge.

Sunday October 5th 1941: At sea. A very nice day today, sunny and warn. There was a church service in the stern, but I was reading in the bows so did not go. During the afternoon I sat on the forecastle and read or played chess with my chums. I also began to write a letter to Monica.

About four we saw three ships, which may have formed part of another convoy, sailing in the opposite direction, right out on the horizon. I saw the leading ship signal by lamp to our cruiser as they went by. In the evening the aircraft carrier left us as we have now passed out of the area of special danger. Though, of course, there is still great danger of U-boats or surface raiders. We need not sleep in our clothes now, according to orders, and, at midnight, the clocks are to be put back an hour. There was hymn singing to the accompaniment of an accordion. This is the first time that I have heard this instrument used in this way. I believe this is all the news for today so Good Night to all my loved ones and God Bless You.

During tea time there was a collection for the widow of the gunner that died on Friday. The chaps turned up well and quite a large amount was collected.

Monday October 6th 1941: At sea. Dawn was a little before seven, and I went on deck to view it. Overhead a few paling stars remained of night and, towards the East, a streak of light broke through the bank of clouds which darkened the horizon. In a few minutes the sky lightened and, above the black mass of clouds, appeared the red light of a new day.

Soon I could see the masts and funnels of the following ships, while the fighting tops of the cruiser were silhouetted against the lightening sky. Then the outline of our neighbours could be seen, hurrying over the water with their bow waves whitening their black hulls. So was born October 6th 1941, and I went below to breakfast. The warm wind of darkness gave way to a strong wind which made me take shelter behind a deck house in the bows. I stayed there, reading in comfort, until lunch was ready. There are oranges to be bought in the canteen, but not for me, as I sent home or spent all of my pay before I came aboard.

Tuesday October 7th 1941: At sea. The day began by raining but after lunch the sun came out and it became very hot. We had boat drill again in the afternoon. I have got a good idea of getting some money. I am returning empty bottles that fellows are too lazy to take back to the canteen and getting tuppence on each! In the evening I continued to write up my letters home until bedtime. It was so hot that it was after eleven before I, at last, went to sleep. I hope that soon I can change into my tropical dress.

Wednesday October 8th 1941. At sea. We began navigation and signals today and I quite enjoyed the lessons. I finished my letters home, and put them in the bag by the Orderly Room. I do hope they arrive safely. I am looking forward to hearing from home as well. Very little to write about. I took a walk on deck in the moonlight before turning in and the sight was very pleasing.

Letter dated 5th to 8th October 1941 - At sea.

Sweet love,

Goodness knows when I will be able to post this letter, but, if we touch port, I may be able to send this to you. I am sure you want to know how I am getting along on this voyage. I cannot tell you the name of the ship I am on, or any details of the convoy, but I may say that I have very good quarters. The sea was roughish during the first three days, and lots of the fellows were sick. I did not feel too good on the first day. Will you be a dear and save the envelopes that my letters come in. Some may not have postage stamps on them, but are likely to have official rubber stamp impressions on them. They will make a good show in my collection after this war. Dawn was a little

*before seven this morning and I went up on deck to view
it. I have often read accounts of dawn at sea, but it must
be seen to realise the full beauty of the scene. It is hot
tonight, we must be going South at a good speed. I must
finish this letter soon, as mail is being collected on
Wednesday.*

*We are changing into tropical kit this afternoon as it is
becoming very hot. The sea today is so calm that it is like
sailing on a lake, and the water is deep blue, with the tips
of each wave whitened as the wind hits each crest. As
evening falls I must bring this letter to a close and I hope
to be able to write again before long. I hope all is well at
home.*

Your loving husband, Leslie.

Thursday October 9th 1941: At sea. Very hot, but enjoyable.
Nothing to note except that we had navigation lessons in the
morning and signals after lunch. I also had a haircut and shampoo
and played cards or read during my free time. There was a
concert below decks at 20.15hrs but the room was so hot and
crowded that I did not go.

Friday October 10th 1941: At sea. After breakfast I walked
towards the bows and, as I looked towards the other ships, I
saw that a small tramp steamer had come abeam of us. What
surprised me was that on its foredeck was lashed a railway
locomotive! I sat for a time reading when one of the boys said
that quite a number of flying fish were in the water. On looking
over the side for a time I saw lots of small fish leap out of the
water as the ship's bow cut through the waves, and glide as far
as thirty yards. The sun was shining and the rays made them
glisten blueish-green. They reminded me of the Kingfishers on
Alverstone River at home. An hour's navigation passed very
quickly before lunch, and also the signal class later. I am quite
glad to go, even when they are voluntary, as they not only help

me to learn more about my job, but also pass the time away. Spent most of the evening playing Solo with the boys. The weather is lovely and I do wish that Monica and Noel could be with me to enjoy the sun, for now, at home, it will be wet and cold. Oh I do hope to be back in England very soon! God protect my loved ones from danger while I am away, and always.

Today I was issued with emergency rations, and mosquito cream and tablets for purifying water.

Saturday October 11th 1941. At sea. These days I am always in a sweat. It runs in rivers from my brow and down my back, but I have soon got used to it. Should be at Freetown on Tuesday. Two lessons, as usual, during morning and afternoon. Played cards from after tea to bed time. We have been joined by another cruiser and two or three more destroyers.

Sunday October 12th 1941: North Atlantic Ocean. As there were no lessons today I spent most of the day reading. We had iced water at lunch and I sucked away all the ice at the bottom of the jug! After this I went to sleep until tea time. Played Housey-Housey on the deck, until it got dark. There is little or no twilight before darkness. As I took a last walk round the deck before turning in, I saw, on the near horizon, flashes of lightening. As usual, blew kisses home before going to sleep. Clocks were put back another hour tonight.

Monday October 13th 1941: At sea. A gale hit us last night and the men sleeping on the deck were soaked. The ship tossed about a little, but I fell asleep before it passed. This morning the sun is shining and the sea is still. The convoy was met by a Sunderland flying-boat early in the day, which, I believe, will escort us into Freetown. Saw a school of porpoises leaping out of the water very close to the ship's bows. There must have been fifty in number! Navigaton lesson today was on the use of the Dalton computer. The Medical Officer also gave us a talk on keeping fit while out here in hot countries.

Tuesday October 14th 1941: Off Freetown. At five minutes to noon I had my first view of the coast of Africa. Far away, almost lost in the heat mist, appeared the point of a high range of hills. I sat in the bows, watching our approach, and so missing a signalling lesson. After dinner we were nearly in the bay. All ships were moving into line ahead. In the water young dolphins played in the mirror-like surface. Then the palms and houses could be seen, and a steep river ran down the hills behind Freetown. From the ship, the town looked clean and modern. I was a little surprised to see a train passing slowly through the trees. I could see people waving from the shore and, as we passed the shipping in the harbour, each vessel cheered us, which we all returned.

Two ships flying the tricolour also joined in this salute. Anchor was dropped near to the shore and, soon, native boats were alongside. Scores of natives dived for coins thrown from the ship, and seldom missed any, others had fruit for sale. I bought six bananas for sixpence and bargained for an African penny in exchange for two English ones. Apples, peaches, coconuts and melons were also offered for sale. There were two Sunderland flying boats moored in the harbour and another landed as I watched. Some of the sergeant pilots will disembark here. They are to fly Curtis Tomahawks into Egypt.

A small ship was sunk so that her hull was below water. I wonder how she got like that? Tonight we lay with Slave Island on the Port side and the main land on the other. There is no blackout tonight and it is unusual to see the lights in the town, and all the ships of the convoy lit up. There was a cool wind blowing from the shore, which was very pleasing. Almost before we stopped, a water carrier was alongside discharging her cargo into our ships tanks. I managed to take two snaps which I hope come out well. On the right of us, a new jetty or dock is being built. Small charges are shot off at times. To the left are four or five oil storage tanks. A little before sunset we must wear long trousers and put cream on our hands and faces to prevent mosquito bites. I trust all at home are well and happy and soon receive my letters, and that I hear from them too.

Wednesday October 15th 1941: Freetown. We are still in the harbour at Freetown and it was lovely and cool on deck early this morning. It was only just dawn, and the rays of the rising sun lit up the slopes of the hills behind the town. I took a snap of the view and I hope it comes out well.

After breakfast the canoes were alongside offering their goods for sale. I bought a number of limes to suck, as the weather makes me thirsty and all the water is warm. The day passed lazily away and, as night drew on, the sun could be seen sinking quite speedily behind the palms.

Thursday October 16th 1941. Freetown. At navigation lessons today our teacher told us that the Germans are kept on their course, when attacking our cities, by two radio beams from their home bases. He went on to say that, during one raid on Liverpool, we managed to bend these rays, and with the help of the Home Guard, who lit fires on some hills in North Wales, led them to drop their bombs on the hills between Ruthin and Rhyl, believing it to be Liverpool. He also told us that the Radio Location apparatus in British aircraft is housed in a strong metal container equipped with an explosive device. This is to prevent the apparatus falling into enemy hands. The ship is laying opposite to a native village called Clive Town. Scores of the canoes have the address of the owner painted on the side in the native version of English, or in their own language.

Friday October 17th 1941: Freetown. Still in the estuary of the river by Freetown. Hot, as usual, and the sweat runs from me. Except for lessons, the day passes slowly. An oiler came alongside during the morning and refuelled the ship. There were two monkeys playing about on her deck, much to the amusement of us all. An Empire flying boat landed today, and I could see the difference in design of the tail between it and the Sunderland.

The canoes used by the native divers are very light and well made, but those of the traders are old and ramshackle. Fruit prices range from one penny for a banana to six pence for a coconut. They give change quite well, and often put extra fruit in for the person pulling up the basket. One soldier put a broken wrist watch and two packets of cigarettes, which cost him eight pence, in the basket. He received in exchange four or five coconuts and about two dozen bananas. I thought that he did not do too badly! I have not seen any seagulls all the time we have been here, and only one or two other birds. I have seen a number of yellow butterflies, about three inches across, flying about the ship. Instead of navigation lessons today we had an armament lesson on the theory of sighting. I found it very interesting.

Saturday October 18th 1941: Freetown. Spent the morning in the sun, watching the natives selling fruit, and was too lazy to do anything else. We may leave here on Monday, but I hope it will be before, as I am fed up being here. A native passed in his canoe with a number of fish I could not recognise, which he had caught on a line. He called out to me, seeing I was interested in his catch, that he would sell me a line, if I wanted one. Of course, I had to refuse, but I tossed him two coppers instead.

I was talking to one of our boys last night and it came out that he had been transferred from the army and, at one time, had been stationed at Niton Undercliffe. It was jolly to talk about the Island. He knew the Lewis family at Whitwell, of course, I also know them as their daughter used to work at Kern Farm, and those at Lake, who live in Alfred Road, just behind us in Louis Road. Mrs Lewis did Monica's housework when Baby was born, but, of course, we paid her.

Sunday October 19th 1941: Freetown. Spent a little time in the sun this morning as there are no lessons today. The liner laying near to us is called *Alanzoria* and was lowering a boat when the rope at one end broke, and that end fell into the water. I do not think anyone was in it at the time, but some of the gear was washed out. Luckily, the natives in their canoes, rescued it and handed it back through the portholes. A sailor climbed down into the boat and soon put a new rope on.

We left Freetown in the early afternoon and I was asleep at the time, but I woke up as we passed out of harbour. As we went by the *Albatross* we saw the sailors waving to us, a salute which we returned. Little's brother is on this ship, and we went to see him while we were in port. There is a lighthouse, marked black and white, on the other side to Freetown. About six ships turned South as soon as the convoy was out to sea, but the greater part kept West, turning South East later on. Two vessels are flying the French flag. One was named *Prince Balquin* and is a single funnel motor vessel.

Monday October 20th 1941: At sea. A little excitement took place this morning when the corvette on our starboard side began releasing depth charges, and all vessels increased speed as well as hooting with their whistles. As nothing else happened I was inclined to believe it was only a practice, but for later events. I managed to get a large piece of ice at lunch time, and I squeezed two oranges on ice and it made a lovely drink. About 17.30hrs one of the destroyers let off a warning wail, which was taken up by all vessels. Then the fun began. All ships scattered, and no two boats were going in the same direction or at the same speed. The *Duchess of Richmond* led the way, going right up to about twenty-seven knots.

The destroyer nearest to us began firing depth charges at full rate, and immense columns of water were shooting up into the air, right and left, Other destroyers rushed to the spot, and joined in the work. It was thrilling to watch these bloodhounds of the sea fighting for us, but, by now, the scene of the action was so far behind that I could not see if the U-boat was sunk or not. As the destroyers sped back to their places we all joined in a hearty cheer as they passed us. From these events I should judge that the foe must have got wind of the departure of the convoy from Freetown, and waited outside for a chance to attack. I hope the Navy put paid to the submarine, or else he will try again later on. It was peculiar that I felt the love my sweet wife has for me, when I was in some little danger, as strong then as if she were an my arms telling me so. God grant that we soon can be reunited early next year.

Tuesday October 21st 1941: Gulf of Guinea. The clocks were advanced one hour last night. In spite of this I was up at ten past four, and washed and shaved before going back to bed. During navigation this morning someone switched the radio on so we listened to the news from London. Just as our instructor resumed the lesson, the guns started practice, so he told us to pack up.

Wednesday October 22nd 1941: Equator 0 degrees West. We 'crossed the line' today, and at 2 o'clock King Neptune came aboard, with his Court. A number of fellows were charged with odd crimes and sentenced. This was carried out by first covering their faces, and the greater part of their bodies, with lather, which was shaved off by a gigantic wooden razor. To complete all this they were washed down by hosepipe, during which the spectators always got as wet as the victim! The proceedings were livened up when someone turned another hose on old Neptune and washed him off his throne. By the time it was over, everyone was drenched, but hot and happy, so it was a jolly afternoon.

Thursday October 23rd 1941: South Atlantic Ocean. It is not now so warm as it was in Freetown. In fact, it is like crossing from Ryde to Portsmouth on an October day, instead of being on the Equator. Spent more of this afternoon writing up my notes of the navigation and armaments lessons that I have been to on this voyage. In the evening I went to a concert, which the fellows got up, and enjoyed it very much. One chap sang some sentimental songs, which made me think of home, and long to be back with Monica.

Friday October 24th 1941: South Atlantic Ocean. Armament lesson this morning for half an hour or so. The instructor told us that the Germans have a good number of Blenheim Mark 1 aircraft, which they have been using against us. There is a rumour that, when we use our practice morse buzzers, the cruiser has been picking it up on her underwater submarine detector, so we are not likely to use them again. I was paid ten shillings today as a sort of pocket money for the voyage.

Saturday October 25th 1941: South Atlantic Ocean. The weather is quite cold today, which, I was told, is very unusual in this latitude. In the afternoon I went to the films, which were held in the Officers mess room. There were two shorts, and a main one, 'Convict 99' starring Will Hay. It was funny, but quite impossible, as all his films are, but I enjoyed it no end.

Sunday October 26th 1941: South Atlantic Ocean. Up early and washed, then went back to bed until after seven. Spent most of the afternoon writing home. I finished the one to Monica but have only got half way through Mother's. I saw three sharks swimming just under the water by the bows of the ship, so that their dorsal fins cut out of the water. They soon made off. Tonight the moon is almost overhead and clocks are advanced another half an hour at midnight. Played chess and cards until bedtime.

Monday October 27th 1941: South Atlantic Ocean. Quite cold today so I have been wearing my blue trousers and jacket. I watched a few boxing rounds in the afternoon, before hearing a lecture by the MO on the effects of flying. King Neptune presented me with a certificate to say that I had Crossed The Line. I have found out that our ship, the *Duchess of Richmond*, is code named HM Transport B3.

Tuesday October 28th 1941: South Atlantic Ocean. Quite cold today, and little to note. I watched the boxing and tug-of-war during the afternoon. Played chess in the evening. Navigation classes as usual.

Wednesday October 29th 1941: South Atlantic Ocean. We have PT each morning, for half an hour or so, but, with the ship lurching as it did, it was impossible to do with any success today. The ship is approaching the Cape and the sea is becoming quite high and the wind is increasing. Spent most of my time reading and writing up my notes.

Thursday October 30th 1941: South Atlantic Ocean. I sat in the bows this morning and, as the sea ran high, it was like being on a see-saw. The wind blew strong so I put on a pullover, yet still felt a slight chill. Saw an Anson aircraft flying about. A few birds were flying round us, and four small ones were snow white. They were not gulls for they were obliged to flap their wings continuously, and were too small. There were gulls, but these were larger than the average English sea bird. Their bodies were white but the colour of wings varied from black to light brown. About nine this morning we passed a small boat that looked like a Coaster, travelling in the opposite direction, and being tossed about like a cork. There was an argument as to what flag she was flying, as some said it was Belgian and others said the Union of South Africa. A little before tea I was called on deck by the boys to see land away on the port horizon. After tea we were close in to land, only about twenty miles out, and part of the convoy was making for it. The most prominent feature was a flat mountain, enshrouded in clouds at the top, and a pointed mountain alongside. We guessed this must be Cape

Town, but it was settled by a member of the crew who told us that the mountain was definitely Table Mountain, and that we were less than twenty miles away. By dark we had left the Cape behind.

Friday October 31st 1941: At sea. We must be getting near to Durban, as the powers that be have taken a list of how much money we want changed into African coinage. We went down to the hold to get our kit bags in the morning, but they are not out yet, so we must wait until tomorrow. Only eight of the boys turned up for armaments class, so the Instructor told us jokes instead.

Saturday November 1st 1941: At sea. Cold, and it rained for most of the day. We have been told that we are to disembark in our blue uniform, so I changed from khaki during the afternoon. No more lectures on the *Duchess of Richmond*. Saw my kit being brought out of the hold in preparation for going ashore. We were met by an armed Merchant Cruiser during the afternoon. I received ten shillings pay and handed in two pounds to be changed into African money.

Sunday November 2nd 1941: Off Durban. The day began as yesterday, wet and chilly. At times the rain mist lifted and I got a view of the coast, a high hilly land which invited one to look over the peaks to see what lay beyond. The convoy arrived off Durban about half past three in the afternoon. The Merchant Cruiser dashed in but soon sent out a message by lamp which turned the convoy out to sea again. It seems that we arrived too late for the tide, and must wait until tomorrow before we can enter the harbour. The Merchant Cruiser is a very swift craft and well armed, having at least ten quick firing guns. It is a nuisance having to spend another night at sea, as we have handed in our blankets and must do without them tonight.

It is a lovely night, the moon is all but full, the sky clear of cloud, and a slight wind blowing, just enough to freshen. If the vessel was only back on its old job of carrying people on pleasure bent, and my dear wife was with me, I would have all I desire. God bless her and all at home. It was on nights just like this that we used to sit on the cliff at Shanklin and talk of many things when I was courting her. We have been very happy together, so please God look after Monica and baby Noel and let him grow up into a pleasant and clever youth. Tonight we talked of books and the possibilities of inter-planetary flying.

Monday November 3rd 1941: Durban. A lovely hot day today and soon the bay of Durban was in sight. We entered about twelve, and dropped anchor about half a mile from the shore. The rest of the convoy was escorted in by a battleship. From the deck Durban looks a clean, modern city, with miniature sky scrapers along the waterfront. The hills to the right of the town remind me very much of the Island on a summer afternoon. After lunch the vessel began to move into the bottleneck entrance of the docks. We passed the breakwater with its mobile crane running along its length. After two hours of moving and turning in the narrow channel we, at length, docked safely. As we passed, people on the shore and ships, cheered us. One Liner was loaded with native troops, with whom we exchanged greetings. There were two Hospital ships in the harbour, as well as another Merchant Cruiser.

Some of the boys threw coppers to the natives on shore, and there was quite a scramble for them. At about six we were given passes to see Durban and, a few minutes later, we were ashore. Four of us made up our party, Jim Banyer and two others, whose names I have forgotten, and myself. We got two rickshaws, pulled by natives dressed in white, and very smart they looked with their white plumes. Around their ankles they wore bells which rang as they ran. They took us right into the centre of the city for only sixpence each, though one did try to overcharge us at first.

I only had tuppence ha'penny, but Jim lent me two shillings until I get my notes back. We saw the City Hall and Cenotaph, both are very fine in design, though I only saw them at night. The streets are very well lit, having two different coloured lights, blue and yellow. The shops were built in arcades which, as it showered for a short time, were most useful. Though the shops, for the greater part, were shut, all had their lights on. The streets were full, mainly with troops. We had a meal of two eggs, chips, coffee and biscuits for seven shillings and three pence for all four of us! We enjoyed the food very much. Then we walked around the town and I bought some South African postage stamps, for my collection, from the machine outside the General Post Office.

We bought a dozen oranges for nine pence, and some chocolate. Sweets and chocolates are much dearer than they are at home, but much more plentiful. About ten we began to walk back to the ship, but got lost as usual, and had to ask the way. Even then we took the wrong turning because we landed in the middle of a railway junction. After crossing a dozen sets of rails, and dodging two trains, we came upon one of the old reversible electric locomotives. At last we reached the other side, and we were soon on board the old B3, alias the *Duchess of Richmond*. It was not long before I blew my kisses and love home, and fell asleep. It was just after 2300hrs.

Tuesday November 4th 1941: Durban. I was lucky to get shore leave from 1300hrs today, so I put my doll mascot in my belt and sallied forth. The four of us took a taxi to the Post Office where I sent cables home to let Monica and Mother know that I was alright. They only cost half-a-crown each. Then we went for a walk around the city, making purchases as we went. I bought a book of 'photos of Durban, which are being sent to Monica. I hope she receives them before Xmas. I also got three books to read on the train journey tomorrow. Then we were told that we could travel on the buses and trams free and, if we took a certain bus, we could go a round journey in the town, lasting about half an hour. This we did, and enjoyed it very much.

I saw many flowers; pretty and of bright colouring. One tree had a bloom like a very large poppy growing from it's branches, while another was covered with a small blue flower and was without leaves. Most gardens had hedges of flowering shrubs. When we arrived back at the City Hall we had a large tea at the YMCA. Then we split up, Jim and Douglas went to see the opera called *Faust* but, as I know it off by heart, Don and myself went to the Metro. The film was called 'Doctor Jekyl and Mr Hyde'. It was very good indeed. We got a rickshaw to take us back to the ship, but the silly fool did not know the way, so we picked up a merchant sailor who directed us there. Jim and Doug were back a little before us, and they too enjoyed their evening out.

Wednesday November 5th 1941 - Guy Fawkes Day: Durban. We began disembarking about nine this morning. It was a scurry and scramble, but at least we were all off the ship, and standing with our kit on the quay. Then we piled into the waiting train. As we moved off, we were handed sacks of oranges, and we had about four each. There are only 117 of us, so we are quite a small jolly party. To describe the passing country is beyond my scope, but I managed to take a few photos, which I hope come out well. We passed the native preserve of The Valley of a Thousand Hills. The sight was most pleasing, with the Kraals built on the sloping sides of the hills. Most of the high land is a plateau. The train was electric, and we travelled at a good speed, winding up and up into the hills. We passed through Pietermaritzburg, Tweedie, Tims River, Lidgetton, Nottingham, Road, Newdell, Frere, Hartshill and then we arrived at Ladysmith.

We stopped for a short time here, but soon we were on our way once more. I turned in on one of the six bunks in our compartment and, after blowing home my kisses, I fell asleep.

Thursday November 6th 1941: Lyttelton. I was up about ten to six and, after washing and dressing, went into the Dining Car for breakfast. The meals are very fine on the train and we all like them. The train is now being pulled by a steam locomotive. Jim told me that the change over was made at about three this morning. At a little after nine we arrived at a smallish place called Lyttelton, which was our destination. From the railway station we travelled by a comfortable lorry to the South African Air Force camp near by. After being issued with two blankets, pillow and case, mug, and some soap, we began filling in more forms. Then it began to rain very hard, and turned the dusty roads into a muddy bog. We were then free for the day, and we went in for lunch. The meal was very nice, and the chef gave me much more than I was able to eat. Natives wait on us during the meals here. At four, Jim, Doug, Don, and myself went into Roberts Heights. We were given a lift in a car by an officer, who picked up two other South Africans, as we went along. He asked us where we were going so we told him that we had some laundry with us we wanted doing. He very kindly took us to the Pretoria Garrison Institute, where we left it, after buying some clothes hangers. The place is quite small, but I must look over it when we next have time.

On the way back I found a small plant growing wild, in bush like form, and with flowers like those of a sweet pea, but with no scent. A passing car took us along to the corner of the Jo'burg road and, from there, an Army Chaplain, Captain by rank, took us into the camp. He told us many things about Africa, and said that he was going North to join his regiment. We said goodbye to him and thanked him very much. After dinner I unpacked my kit and read a little before going to bed.

Friday November 7th 1941: I took first turn at Orderly. This only means that I stay in the hut all day to see that the natives do not enter and steal anything. The SAAF is run on the same lines as the South African Army. I was issued with rifle no. 37141 as 'A' Flight is responsible for mounting guards during the coming week. In the evening Don and myself went up to the Milk Bar, which is in the camp, and had a glass of milk for one penny and a bottle of Kokalade, which is a drank made of chocolate, for three pence. The sky was filled with stars, and the Southern Cross was pointed out to me.

Saturday November 8th 1941: Must note that yesterday I sent two cables home from the camp Post Office. We had half an hour's rifle drill this morning and then we were photographed for our log books. This was the end of the days programme and, as we were free, I spent the rest of the afternoon sorting my kit out.

Sunday November 9th 1941: Johannesburg. After church parade Ginger Gibson, from the next bungalow, went out of camp. Our whole flight, about 36 of us, are confined to camp, being the duty flight. But no one took any notice and only the eleven men on actual guard duty stayed in! We walked to the crossroads, a distance of about three miles, and from there a 2nd Lieutenant and his father took us into Jo'burg. We had lunch at a soldiers club for sixpence, before going on a tram to the zoo. All travel on the buses or trams is free for servicemen, as it was in Durban.

After looking round the birds and animals we sat down in the shade of a tree to rest as the sun was most hot. A couple, who were sitting nearby, offered us cigarettes and entered into conversation with us. After a while they asked us to join them for a cup of tea at the zoo cafe, which we did. Then they took us down to see the boating lake and to listen to the band. Later they asked us if we would care to have dinner with them. As we expected, they rang up their house to say that we were coming. We all went by train to Kensington, where they lived. We had an excellent meal and talked a great deal about Africa. Their name is Weed and they have been in Transvaal since the end of the last war. He is an electrical engineer working for the railway. They introduced us to their son, who is working for his father, but has not yet completed his exams. Two of their friends called to see them, and we were introduced to them. They had been in Africa for 21 years and are quite old.

Mr Weed rang up the station to find out the time of the trains back to Lyttlelton. One was due at ten so they took us down to catch it in their car, and saw us off from the platform. It was about twenty to twelve before I got back into camp.

Letter dated 9th November 1941 from LAC L. Harris at 75 Air School S.A.

My own love,

I miss you, my love, and think only of the happy days we had before I joined the RAF, and of the return to them, if all goes well, when peace at last rests in shell-blasted Europe. I spent an afternoon in Durban, and enjoyed it no end. It was from the General Post Office that I sent the cable to you and brought some stamps for my collection. It does not cost anything for me to send letters to you, so this will be a great saving for me, and I understand you can send letters to me for 1½ pence instead of 2½ pence.

I should have liked you to have been with me, for there were a great number of interesting things to see. I have taken a number of photos and, when I get them developed, I will see if I am able to send them to you.

We travelled to Lyttleton via Ladysmith, and a very comfortable journey it was. We spent a night sleeping in bunks, and very well I slept. It is very hot now, so I will close this short letter, and write again when I know more about this place.

Your ever loving husband, Leslie.

Monday November 10th 1941: Johannesburg. Sent some newspapers home and wrote a note to the Weeds to thank them for the good time they gave us yesterday. We had an hour's drill this morning followed by some training films. This was all the programme for today, and as we had the afternoon free I went over to Johannesburg by myself. Ginger said that the Weed family were too dull for him and he has gone off with some of the boys to Pretoria to look for girls. The Weed family were pleased to see me and took me to the films. There was a stage show of seven items, and as the programme was long, we came out before the end to enable me to catch the 11pm train. I got a lift to the station in a passing car and just managed to catch the train, but without a ticket. I paid on the train but it cost me another shilling for a booking fee. Mr Weed has lent me a book on South Africa., which was kind of him, and I will return it the next time I go over.

Tuesday November 11th 1941: Roberts Heights. Drill and films again this morning, but nothing else. Don and myself went to Roberts Heights to fetch our clean laundry, but it had not yet arrived, so we just left some more to be done and then returned to camp. The two minutes silence was held at 11am. I was on duty as part of the Motor Transport guard from 2200hrs to 2359hrs.

Wednesday November 12th 1941: Lyttelton Camp. On guard again from 0400hrs to 0600hrs. It rained a little, but I was under cover all the time. I had two more guard periods, from 1000hrs to 1200hrs and 1530hrs to 1730hrs. During the last guard a dust cloud blew up and I had to take cover in my box. For a few minutes nothing could be seen, just the dust blowing along. Then it cleared very quickly. I have a pass until midnight, but, as I did not come off guard until 1730hrs, I did not feel like going out, so I am doing some sewing to mend my socks. Whilst on sentry go today I saw a black and yellow lizard which could cover the ground at quite a pace. There are a number of flying stick insects which appear at night, also some small silver moths similar to those that I have seen at home.

Thursday November 13th 1941: Pretoria. 'A' Flight went clay pigeon shooting this morning and I was very pleased with myself that I won by one hit. In the early afternoon I went to Roberts Heights to fetch my laundry, which cost three shillings and sixpence – rather a lot, I thought. Ken, George and myself went to Pretoria in the evening, where we went to the 20th Century Cinema to see the film 'Lady Hamilton'. It was jolly good and showed how a good man (Nelson) was ruined by a woman. We just had time for a quick look round the city before we took the train back to Kloofzicht.

We saw Kruger's statue and were told that once someone painted him red and put a bucket on his head. We also saw the Parliament buildings. It only cost seven pence single to Kloofzicht, which is a little nearer to the camp than Lyttelton.

Friday November 14th 1941: Lyttelton Camp. I sent Christmas cards home to Monica and Mother. I do hope they all have a Happy Christmas. I went on guard again at 3.30pm and took over MT guard from 1800hrs to 2000hrs. Nothing else of note.

Saturday November 15th 1941: Johannesburg. On MT guard again from 0000hrs to 0200hrs. All quiet. I spent the rest of the morning getting ready to go to Johannesburg this afternoon, if all goes well. George Cribben and myself left on the 1.45pm train, arriving in Jo'burg a little after three. We had tea and chocolate eclairs before calling on the Weed family. We all stayed for (our second) tea and then four of us (Mr and Mrs Weed stayed at home) called for another RAF fellow and his girl, before going in their car to the films. The picture was called 'Singapore Woman' and was poorish. It was about half past twelve before we had a cup of coffee at their house and returning to the city, so we slept in the City Hall, which is fitted up for that purpose.

I enjoyed the day, but I should have enjoyed it a thousand fold if Monica and Baby were with me.

Sunday November 16th 1941: Kensington. George and myself were up early today and after washing we went out for breakfast. We took this meal at the Jewish Service Club and had a jolly good feed for sixpence. We spent the rest of the morning looking round the city and taking a few photos of the main buildings. After lunch we again went to Kensington and we all went walking in Rhodes Park. We talked about the flowers and lots of other things about Africa. Then followed dinner and, later in the evening, we all went on to the veranda, where it was cool. Andrew played some tunes on the bagpipes, but, as he is only learning to play, at times it sounded funny. At a little before ten they took us down to the station and we returned to camp by train.

Monday November 17th 1941: Roberts Heights. Easy day again and we spent all afternoon at Roberts Heights swimming in the garrison pool. While I was there I collected my laundry and left two rolls of film to be developed. Mr Weed is taking another roll to be developed in a shop in Johannesburg. After tea Don and myself skipped camp to go to the films at Pretoria. An Army Captain took us there in his car. We were in quite early so we spent an hour or so looking round. The place is nothing compared with Jo' burg. We saw an old film called 'The Mark of the Vampire' at a cafe sort of place. We did not have to pay an entrance fee but we ordered a cup of milk each, which cost one and six, so, no wonder they did not charge to go in! We missed the early train so we had to wait on the station for the 11.25pm for Kloofzicht. We were in camp before midnight.

Tuesday November 18th 1941: Roberts Heights. Just half an hour's drill this morning, followed by another film show, as yesterday, was all we did this morning. We all slept from ten until lunchtime. Bye the bye, the South Africans call their cinemas Bioscopes! We went swimming at Roberts Heights again this afternoon, and found the water very warm. I did not go out this evening, but wrote letters home, and then went to bed early. I do so hope that everything is getting along alright at home and that all are well and happy.

Letter dated 18th November 1941 *from LAC L. Harris at 75 Air School S.A.*

Dearest Love,

I am getting along here well, but my, it is hot at times. It is so bad that after ten in the mornings we have done nothing at all. Don and myself went to Pretoria yesterday to have a look round at the old capital of the Boer Republic. We saw the statue of Kruger outside the railway station and the workmanship of it was so good that I was sorry that I did not have my camera with me to take a photo of it, but if I get over again I will take it with me. We walked around the city seeing many buildings of beauty in design. Pretoria is a much older place than Johannesburg and there is not so much of interest. Some of the boys went to the zoo there, but I did not, but may the next time I go in.

There is a swimming pool at Roberts Heights, a small township a few miles away, and yesterday and today we have been there for a swim. The water is lovely and warm. I do wish that you were with me for in England now the weather must be cold and wet. Even so, I would much rather be back with you, my dear wife, than out here in this sunny climate. There was another dust storm this afternoon and dust blows into our bungalows and everything, including our beds, become covered with it. I will be sending some films to you soon I hope, as I left a roll to be developed and they will be ready by Friday. I do not seem to be able to think of anything to write about out

here. I cannot write about the work I am doing but I will
have so much to tell you about when we are together
again.

Good night and God bless both of you.

Your husband and lover, Leslie.

Wednesday November 19th 1941: Lyttelton Camp. The wind
this morning was a little chilly, but as the sun got up, it became
warm again. The time before lunch was spent in the usual way,
a little drill, films, and then just doing what we liked. I am on
guard tonight at 1730hrs. I also did Main Gate guard from 2200hrs
to 2400hrs and again, on the 20th, from 0400hrs to 0600hrs.

***Letter dated 19th November 1941** from LAC L. Harris*
at 75 Air School SA

My own sweet wife,

I am beginning this letter this morning as I have some
spare time, but I do not think I will post it until I have
some more news to tell you. Things here are a little slow so
far, but we all hope to get a move on with our work very
soon now. The camp here is not too bad, and is more or
less self contained so we do not go out of camp to buy
anything we want very often. It is so peaceful here that
war does not seem to be in this land at all. I am awaiting
your letters to know what is happening at home, and hope
they arrive very soon. You must tell me all about Noel and
his doings, because I so miss his funny little ways. It is
sunny and hot today and every thing is dry and dusty. I
have seen some very pretty flowers, both wild and
cultivated. I hope to be able to bring some seeds back with
me to see if they will grow at home. The pocket case you
gave me is most useful as I now have a number of stamps
for my collection. One of the South Africans has given me

a lot of stamps from the Belgian Congo. There is so little to write about that I will close now, but will write a longer letter over the weekend.

Your loving husband, Leslie.

Thursday November 20th 1941: Johannesburg. Came off guard at six this morning and after breakfast went to sleep until just after ten. Jim and myself went up to Roberts Heights to take some laundry into the PGI. We returned on the mail van. As I had the rest of the day free, because I was on guard yesterday, and Don was on 48 hours sick leave, we decided to go over to Jo'burg. We had to skip camp but managed to get out just after eleven. One of the SA sergeants gave us a lift to the crossroads in his car, though he must have known that we had no right to be out at that hour. The only trouble was that the car stopped at the bottom of the hill and we had to push it to the top before we could get it to start again. There were two Vultures by the roadside that the sergeant pointed out. They flew away as the car approached.

We soon got a lift into Jo'burg, where we had lunch before taking a look round the shops. We hoped to buy one or two small gifts for Christmas, but after two hours were unable to find anything suitable. We went to an afternoon matinee at the 20th Century Cinema. The film was 'Western Union' and it was jolly good. Afterwards we had tea, and decided to part, each going to our own friends in town. I rang up Mrs Weed to ask if I could go over and she agreed. As usual I travelled by tram car, and was soon in Clacton Road. I spent a pleasant evening playing cards with the family and, a little after ten, they took me to the railway station in their car and I returned to camp.

Friday November 21st 1941: Pretoria. Douglas and myself went over to Pretoria after dinner. While we were looking around we met two privates in the South African Army who we spoke to and who showed us round the town. Later we all went to see the film 'The Girl in the News'. It was an English film and was quite good. We returned to camp on the 11.25pm train, and were in bed by midnight.

Saturday November 22nd 1941: Pretoria. As this afternoon is our free day, Doug and myself went over to Pretoria again. After a time Doug made friends with an Army girl so, as I did not want to play Gooseberry, I returned to camp. There I was just in time to meet Jim as he came off guard duty. We decided to go back to Pretoria, so this we did. We sat in the square and talked to anyone who stopped to ask us how we liked their country. We met two more SA soldiers, who are very friendly to the British, and we had an enjoyable time with them. We ended up having a good supper together before returning to our camps.

Sunday November 23rd 1941: Pretoria. After church parade Doug, Jim and myself went once more to Pretoria. We had a look over the city and took one or two snaps. After lunch Doug called for his girlfriend and the three of us went for a walk in the Union Buildings Gardens, Doug and the girl walking a long way behind us. By chance we met the two soldiers who we met yesterday. We decided to have dinner together, after which the six of us sat and talked until it was time for us all to return to our respective camps.

Letter dated 23rd November 1941 **from LAC L. Harris at 75 Air School SA**

My Darling,

Today being Sunday I have just been to church parade and am now free for the rest of the day. I do so wish that this was a Sunday at home, then we could take baby Noel for a walk in the country, even if the weather is not like it is out here. I miss you very much and am just longing to get back to you, my sweet wife. May God protect you both from all ills, and pray that ere long we will be united once

*more. I have not yet received any letters from you, but
hope to within a day or two. Have you received my letters
safely? The fact that it takes so long for letters to travel
between us is a d--- bother, but if we are always thinking
of each other we are not so very far away. I have not
forgotten once to blow you a kiss each night at ten, and
this brings you nearer to me. There are three snaps
enclosed with this letter, so what do you think of them? I
hope to take some more soon, and will send the best home
to you.*

*A few of us went to Pretoria last night, and met some of
the chaps of the South African Army. They were jolly boys
and showed us round the town. I had my camera with me
and so was able to snap some of the places we visited.
After dinner we all went to the 'bioscope' as they call the
cinema out here. The film was called The Girl in the News
and was not too bad, as it was an English picture. We
returned on the 11.25pm train and were in bed by
midnight. The dust is a bother when it is windy, but the
sun shines all day, and I am getting very brown. The heat
has made my lips crack and they are a little painful at
times. This is all the news today so I will close.*

Au Revoir, your loving husband, Leslie.

Monday November 24th 1941: Roberts Heights. We began
our course today by being issued with books on the subjects
that we shall be studying. They are Photography, Armaments,
Air Reconnaissance and Airmanship. Then we had a lecture on
the political powers in Africa, which I found very interesting. At
four, the three of us, Doug, Jim and myself, went to the PGI at
Roberts Heights to take some rolls of film in for developing.
Both Doug and Jim are being posted on Thursday. I am very
sorry that they are going without me, as we have been together
since Stratford, but if all goes well we may meet again somewhere.
We all stayed in tonight and I wrote home and sent off six
Christmas cards.

Tuesday November 25th 1941: Lyttelton Camp. My feet were so blistered from walking on the hard ground that I reported to the MO and he put some dressings on them. He has also given me two days off to rest them. All the Flight, including myself, were given 50 Springbok cigarettes from the SA Gifts and Comforts Committee, which was jolly good of them. Before lunch Jim and myself went up to Roberts Heights to take some more films in to be developed. About four Douglas and myself went over to Pretoria and had tea at the YMCA. Afterwards Douglas went to a dance and I went to the films. It was at the Opera House and the film was 'Spring Time'. It made me think of Monica and home because we saw it together in England. I caught the 9.45pm bus to Roberts Heights and got a lift back to camp, so was in bed just about half past ten.

Wednesday November 26th 1941: Roberts Heights. Good news, I received a cable from my darling wife. Thank God they are well. I answered it at once by letter. I also received a letter from Jo' burg asking me over for the weekend. I hope to be able to go. I answered it this morning. I also let the SA Army boys know that I would be going to Pretoria tonight, after calling in at Roberts Heights PGI. Douglas and Jim came with me but I lost them at the Army camp so I went to the films with one of the Africans. We went to the 20th Century bioscope and saw a picture called 'One Night in Rio'. It passed the time away, but it was not too good. I nearly missed the train after leaving the Army camp for I had to take a taxi from the square to the station.

Thursday November 27th 1941: Lyttelton Camp. Oh! What a day this has been. It began by waking up to find that 29 of us were under open arrest for being out of camp last night. Only five of our boys stayed in and that because they had no money. We were taken up before the CO but could not all get into the charge room, so some of us sat outside on the step. The 'Old Man' first gave us a lecture on skipping camp and then quashed the charge, saying that next time we would all spend an hour on extra drill! Next we had a navigation lesson, followed by one on armaments. By then it was time for morning tea. We should have had a maths lesson, but the Officer arrived late and then he could not find any log tables. Eventually he told us to clear off, but not before he gave us a cigarette each, to make up for those he scrounged from us yesterday. To finish the morning we were supposed to have PT, but as only eleven of us turned up, the sergeant cancelled the class. In the afternoon Jim and Don went to Jo'burg, while I went clay pigeon shooting. I missed twice, but I drew, on points, with two other fellows. Our Officer asked if six of us would volunteer to help out with the Guest Night being held at the Officers Mess that evening.

I went over, with five others, and we had some fun. Sometimes we got the orders mixed up but no one seemed to mind too much, as long as the drinks flowed the guests sorted it out amongst themselves.

At the end, we each had a five course dinner at a small table in a corner of the Mess, our dessert was ice-cream. We were also given a box of cigarettes each, and those that drank got free drinks from the bar. It is now nearly ten and I am just going to bed. There is a hell of a storm raging outside, like nothing I have ever heard before. Hailstones at least half an inch or more across, are tearing down and hitting the iron roof with such noise that it is impossible to hear one speak, unless you shout. Well, I am going to bed now. Good night and bless all at home.

Friday November 28th 1941: Roberts Heights. Lessons again this morning, but after lunch we did very little. Jim left for Port Elizabeth. I am sorry that he has gone as he was my best pal. Douglas is in hospital with 'flu. The CO sent over five shillings for each of the six of us that helped in the Mess last night. We went into Roberts Heights at about 16.30hrs to leave six films to be printed for Jim. I will post them on to him later. I also telephoned Mrs Weed to thank her for asking me over for the weekend. We have lessons at 18.40hrs tonight, which is a bore.

Saturday November 29th 1941: Johannesburg. Don and myself got a lift into Pretoria, from where we went by the 14.00hrs train into Jo'burg. We parted on the way to Kensington, myself calling an the Weeds, while Don went to his friends in Queen's Street. Mrs Weed was out, but Mr Weed and a friend of his, who is a Captain in the Army, made me welcome. Later Andrew and Mrs Weed came back from shopping. After dinner three of us went to the 'Empire' to see (once more for me) 'Target for Tonight'. After the show I said "Goodnight" to them and spent the night at the City Hall.

Sunday November 30th 1941: Johannesburg. Slept well, and was up early. After washing and dressing I had breakfast at the club. Then I got a paper which kept me occupied for an hour or two. I arrived at Clacton Road about 11am. We chatted until lunchtime. During the afternoon we played bridge. Mr Weed and Andrew against a girlfriend of Andrew's and myself. They won by 690 points, mainly due to the girl doubling on a two call. After dinner we played rings, at which I did a little better than the last time I played. Andrew and the girl took me down to the station in their car and I was back in camp before 23.30hrs after a happy weekend.

Monday December 1st 1941: Roberts Heights. This afternoon we went clay pigeon shooting at the butts at the top of the hill. I only hit two out of four, which was not too good. It was another hot South African day and, by the time we got back to camp I was wet with perspiration. I received a letter from private Roberts asking me over to Pretoria next weekend. I replied that I would if I got the time free.

Tuesday December 2nd 1941: Roberts Heights. The Photography Examination was held this morning, but I think that I passed alright. In the afternoon Don and myself got a lift in a car up the long three mile road from Lyttelton Camp to Roberts Heights. I bought some film for my camera at the PGI before returning the same way. After tea I wrote letters home to Monica and Mother before joining the boys for supper in the canteen.

Wednesday December 3rd 1941: Lyttelton Camp. Damn hot and dusty today and I would like to be home with my dear Wife. The Maths Examination was held this morning, but it was very simple after what we had to do in England. A letter arrived for me from Jim at Port Elizabeth. He got there safely and has settled in and is doing well.

Thursday December 4th 1941: Lyttelton Camp. In the evening we had dinner in the Officers Mess. On the way back, in the dark, for in spite of the fact it was only seven, it began to rain and developed into a tropical storm with lightning flashes that I have only seen once before, and that at Freetown. Hail fell in sizes of around a quarter to a half inch in diameter and the storm lasted most of the night.

Friday December 5th 1941: Pretoria. A cable arrived from Monica telling me that all is well at home. In the evening I went out of camp the usual way, by walking out of the main gate when the Orderly Officer was not about. It does not matter about the sentinel because he is one of our boys and knows that we have not got passes. I arrived in Pretoria about six and had to take cover during a heavy rain storm. It did not last long . I went to the 20th Century cinema where the film was 'Rebecca'. It was one of the best shows I have yet seen. I came back by train to Klooffzicht and walked across the fields to the back of the camp where I got in through the barbed wire.

Saturday December 6th 1941: Pretoria. This weekend off again so went to the zoo in Pretoria. It is not so large as the one in Johannesburg but I enjoyed looking at the exhibits. After having tea I went again to the films, this time to the Capitol to see 'Kitty Foile'. There is little else to do in the evening, except see a film, go to a dance, or go drinking. As I neither dance or drink I just go to the bioscope.

Sunday December 7th 1941: Pretoria. War with Rumania, Finland and Hungary as from midnight 6th/7th, Well, the more, the merrier. Once again my idle feet lead me to Pretoria, or, at least, I got a lift into the city. This time I went to the Union Buildings, which I have often seen on postage stamps, not ever thinking that this day I would climb the stone steps into the gardens in which these government offices are set. They lie on a hill just outside the city and, as I stood looking I beheld the whole of Pretoria below me, I thought how much it must have changed since the invading English force first saw it, when Lord Roberts attacked the Boer army here. I took a number of photographs before walking around the flower beds and seeing quite a number of lovely plants for the first time. Later it started to rain heavily so I was obliged to return by tramcar to the Church Square, where I had tea at a cafe before intending to take a bus to Roberts Heights. I realised that I had left my camera in the cafe, but luckily it was still there when I went back for it. After finally arriving at Roberts Heights I was able to get a lift back to camp.

Monday December 8th 1941: Japan has declared war on the USA and Britain. The Japs have bombed Manila and Pearl Harbour causing much destruction and loss of life. It was a dastardly attack without warning. Lessons, PT and drill made up the programme for today, and took on a new meaning.

*Letter dated 8th December 1941 **from LAC L. Harris at Lyttelton Camp, SA***

My own sweet Wife,

I miss you so very much these days as it draws near to Christmas. Oh darling let us pray that next year on Christmas day we will be together to enjoy it. How are you and baby Noel? I do so hope you are both well and happy. I have not yet had any letters from England, but I hope to any day now. I shall cheer like mad when I get a letter from you and read the news from home. I got your second cable on Saturday morning and was so glad that everything is well with you. This country is not too bad, but the heat and dust are the devil at times. One of the main troubles is the price of things here. Everything is three times the price they are at home and the cheapest seats in the cinema are three shillings. I have seen quite a number of large coloured butterflies flying about. They are much larger than our English ones and have much brighter colours. In spite of all this I would give the world to be back in the rain and snow of the Motherland. God bless and protect you both forever. I feel very homesick tonight and live only to settle down in a home of our own and to live our own free lives in peace. What do you think of the news these last few days? At last we are at war with Japan, Finland, Hungary and Romania. I wonder if the USA will declare war against Germany as well and will the Union of South Africa go to war with these four new foes of England? You see, the armed forces here sign on to only fight in Africa so they will not fight in Europe or Asia where the real war is taking place.

I went to Pretoria again this weekend. I have enclosed a snap of one of the places I visited. It is the museum, near to the railway station. I enjoyed myself no end looking over the place. I saw lots of relics of the Boer war and many works of the natives. I was there for some hours and even then I did not see all over it. I hope to go over again one day soon if I can. We may be leaving Lyttelton soon to go to another school in Cape Province on the 18th of the month. It is about a two day journey by train so you see, I am likely to travel about a lot before I at last get back to you and home. The other fellow in the photograph is my chum Jim. He is 28 and is a jolly fine chap and we had a good time together.

Well, my love, I think this is all for now, so, till we meet again. Au revoir sweet wife.

Your lover and husband, Leslie.

Post Script: To Master Noel. I wish you a very very happy first birthday and may you be happy all your life, my little baby son.

Your loving father, Leslie

Tuesday December 9th 1941: Lyttelton Camp. Very cold this morning and it rained slightly, no sunshine all day. The navigation exam was held this afternoon but it was not too bad. However, feeling tired after the effort, I decided to go to bed early.

Wednesday December 10th 1941: Roberts Heights. Went swimming at Roberts Heights pool during this afternoon. The pool is large and has lawns all around it, with trees as its border. There is also a small hut where one can buy lemonade and sweets. Very few people ever go there, in fact our boys are about the only ones who go swimming, except for one or two children. After tea I skipped camp to go into Pretoria by myself, but I got so fed up being alone that I returned on the 8.40pm train and was in bed just after nine. The Royal Navy suffered a severe loss when the *Prince of Wales* and the *Repulse* were sunk by the Japs in the Far East. The fighting in Malaya is becoming very fierce indeed. I doubt if the Yanks will stop the Japs from capturing Guam and perhaps the Philippine Islands as well.

Thursday December 11th 1941: Lyttelton Camp. I had some mangoes for lunch today, but I do not think much of them.

Friday December 12th 1941: Lyttelton Camp. This morning we all went for a so-called route march with our Africaaner sergeant, but it really was just a walk across the Veldt. We went as far as a small dorp (village) called Irene, which is quite a picturesque place. It is almost like a country hamlet in England except instead of cottages there are modern bungalows with gardens full of tropical flowers. On the way, I saw the Black Widow bird, with its two long tail feathers, which, I was told, prevented it from flying in wet weather. Later, beside a small river, I found its nest, built at the end of a thin branch hanging far out over the water. The entrance is under the nest to prevent snakes robbing the birds of their eggs. We returned through a grove of blue gum trees and so, back to Lyttelton. After tea I saw the film called 'Victory' at The Capital bioscope in Pretoria.

Saturday December 13th 1941: Lyttelton Camp. I have a pass which started yesterday at 4pm until midnight tomorrow, but I slept last night in camp. This morning I went into Johannesburg, which is about 32 miles away. I called on the Weeds and spent a jolly day with them. It was after eleven before they drove me from their home in Kensington in their car back into the main city of Johannesburg. I was unable to get a room in the club as it was full, so spent the night in the city hall.

Sunday December 14th 1941: Johannesburg. My wallet was stolen while I was asleep last night. It was a very great loss to me for my dear wife gave it to me. I reported it to the service police and they told me that they would let me know if they ever found it. I spent the morning riding around the city in tramcars. One took me by the 'City Deep' gold mine with its shafts and mountains of waste from the pits. In one place the tram lines are on sleepers, like a railway line. After lunch I went to Kensington where I spent the rest of the day with the Weed family. In the afternoon we went for a walk in the park until teatime. After tea. we played bridge and Mr Weed told tales of Africa until it was time for me to leave to catch the train back to camp.

Monday December 15th 1941: Lyttelton Camp. During this morning we all went out into the veldt and travelled as far as a small place called Fountains. Here we had a cup of tea and some buns before going back for lunch at Lyttelton. As we hope to leave this camp on Thursday, if all goes well. Mrs Weed has asked me to go out to visit them as often as I can before then. Therefore, at about four in the afternoon, I walked down onto the lower Pretoria-Johannesburg road and soon got a lift into the gold mining town of Benoni. From here I got another lift into Kensington. After dinner Mary and her brother took me round to some of their friends where we spent a happy evening. They drove me down to the station just in time to catch the 23.00hrs train.

> *Letter dated December 15th 1941 from LAC L. Harris at Lyttelton Camp SA*
>
> *Sweet love,*
>
> *Just a short note to hope that you are both well and happy. We are leaving here on Thursday to go to Oudtshoorn to continue our training. I am in the middle of packing now so please forgive me for this short note. On Saturday night one of the boys and myself spent the night at one of the clubs in Jo'burg as we were on weekend leave. We shared a room with two South African Air Force men but when we woke up I found my wallet was gone and so was a camera belonging to the other chap. We reported it to the Military Police but I doubt if we will ever hear any more about it. I was sorry to lose it as it was the one you gave to me before we were married and I*

treasured it very much indeed. With it I lost the snaps of you and Baby that I took at home so, dear, if you are able I would like you to send me another photograph of you both. Oh my darling, I love you so and live only for the end of this war when, please God, we can settle down in our own home and live a happy married life as we did before I joined up. Must close now, but will write again very soon. I think it is better to write short letters often rather than just one long one now and again so, if some are lost on the journey to you, the others should, reach you.

So my dearest wife, Au Revoir.

Your ever loving husband, Leslie.

Tuesday December 16th 1941: Johannesburg. As Mrs Weed asked me over again for dinner I went to Johannesburg as early in the afternoon as I could. After tea all five of us went to see the film called 'A Day in Soviet Russia'. I found it very interesting, but sometimes a little dull. I returned on the 23.04 train, for this is the 23.00 from the main station, from Jeppe.

Wednesday December 17th 1941: Johannesburg. Finished packing and then went over to say 'goodbye' and 'thank you' to the Weed family for their kindness to me during my stay in the Transvaal. They all asked me to visit them if ever I am in Johannesburg again. Mrs Weed gave me 100 cigarettes for the journey down to the Cape Province. I was very sorry to say goodbye to them for they are fine friends indeed.

Thursday December 18th 1941: Departing Lyttelton Camp. Left Lyttelton Camp about 12.30hrs and went by lorry to Pretoria. Here, after waiting nearly an hour, we caught the train south. After leaving the city we were out in the wilds with few buildings or trees to be seen. Soon we were crossing the Vaal River into the Orange Free State, which is greener than the Transvaal. It was dusk as we crossed the pretty River Orange and I fell asleep after leaving Bloemfontein.

Friday December 19th 1941: On the train. On through mountainous country we travelled passing Middelburg and Graaff Reinet. The country is almost desert, only small bushes and endless cacti. After leaving Graaff Reinet we were in total desert called the Great Karroo. The meals on the train are very appetising and the bunks on the walls of the compartment are quite comfortable.

Letter dated December 19th 1941. On the train through the Karroo.

My Own Darling Wife,

All my love to you and our little baby Noel. I trust to God that everything is alright at home. No letters have arrived from home yet but there is an English mail in now, so I hope to get some letters from you soon. It is a bit of a job to write when the train is rolling like a ship at sea, but I hope you can read it. Many happy returns of the day to Noel on his first birthday anniversary and may he be all his life as happy as I was a year ago when he was born. It will be jolly to see you both again and to take you both out for walks in the country, as we did during my last leave. When, if all goes well, I at last reach England, we will have the best of all holidays. I am just longing for all the good things you cooked for me. Often in the evening as I go to bed I think of the cheesecakes you used to send me and I feel so homesick. Now I must tell you why I am on this train travelling in the Cape Province. During the last few days of last week we took our examinations at Lyttelton, which, I am pleased to say, I passed OK. Having finished this course we are moving to another flying school about 200 miles from Cape Town, called

Oudtshoorn. I will send you my new address when I know it, but you can write to the old one until then as they will be forwarded.

We left Pretoria at lunch time yesterday and hope to arrive at Oudtshoorn on Saturday morning, so you see, it is quite a long train journey. I enjoy it very much for travelling here is very interesting. The Karroo is more or less desert for no grass will grow there, only a few small bushes. I have taken one or two snaps which I hope to be able to send to you when they are developed. After leaving the Transvaal we crossed the Vaal River into the Orange Free State. The train carried us as we slept through the state and I went to sleep just after we left Bloemfontein. I was up at 4.30 this morning and it is not yet six, so I will stop writing now, but continue later in the day.

Later. We have stopped at a small station for a few moments so I will finish this letter now. As you know, most long train journeys give me a headache, so I do not feel like writing much more so I will close until tomorrow night, when I hope to write to you again.

All my love, your husband, Leslie.

Saturday December 20th 1941: Oudtshoorn. Yesterday was baby Noel's first birthday and I almost forgot the little chap in the rush of travelling. I trust to God. that he is well and happy for always. Arrived at Oudtshoorn at 04.30hrs and the place did not look very inviting in the light of dawn. We were taken by lorry to the camp which is just outside the town. The camp is OK but the town is very small indeed. After lunch we were told that we would not start the course until Monday morning, so Doug, Don and myself went out for a walk. Well, it started as a walk, but a car came along and the driver asked if we wanted a lift. We asked him where he was going and he replied Mossel Bay. We thought this place was about two or three miles away so we thanked him and got in. Well, it turned out it was over fifty miles away and the road ran through a gorge called the Montague Pass and the speed we went down it was great. Mossel Bay is a small seaside town of no great size and the result was we were unable to get rooms for the night. We began by trying to sleep on a wooden seat but it became too cold so we walked down to the railway station and spent the rest of the night in the waiting room.

Letter dated Sunday December 21st 1941
from LAC L. Harris at Oudtshoorn S.A

My Darling One,

My love to you and baby Noel and my hope that we will be together again soon. This is just a short note to tell you of our journey to Mossel Bay, which is about 56 miles away. We left just after lunch and got a lift in a car to this place, taking only a little over two hours on the journey. The country we passed through was of majestic grandeur, for not in the length of England is there a mountain to compare with these Lords of height. Down Montague Pass ran the road giving me views of beauty that I have seen in no other land. On arriving in the town we had supper before going to the films. We were lucky in getting a room for the night, as most were booked for Christmas. The next morning it was raining so we returned on the 10.30 train. It was a very slow journey, but the track ran round the mountains and gave me an opportunity to take a number of photographs which I hope will make good showing. We do not begin lessons until tomorrow so I cannot tell you anything about it yet. The camp is wholly RAF and is much better than Lyttelton, but the town itself is not much. Must close now as it is time for bed, but I will write over Christmas as I have nowhere to go and will be very lonely without you, my darling.

Happy Christmas from your husband Leslie.

No 1335461 L.A.C. L.HARRIS (AIR OBSERVER)
Royal Air Force
Course 15A
No 40 Air School
Oudtshoorn
Cape Province
Sunday December 21st 1941   South Africa

My Darling Own

        My love to you, and baby Noel, and my hope
that we will be together again soon. This is just a
short note to tell you of our journey to Mossel Bay
which is about 56 miles away.

        We left just after lunch and got a lift in a
car to this place taking only a little over two hours of
the journey. The country we passed through was of majestic
grandeur for not in the length of England has a county,
a mountain to compare with these lords of height.
Down Montagu Pass ran to road giving me views
of beauty that I have seen in no other land.

        On arriving in the town we had supper before
going to the films. We were lucky in getting a room
for the night as most were booked for Xmas.

        The next morning it was raining so we returned
on the 10.30 train. It was a very slow journey, but the
way the track ran round the mountains gave me an
opportunity to take a number of photographs which
I hope will make good showing.

        We don't begin lessons until tomorrow so I

Sunday December 21st 1941: Oudtshoorn. By morning we were fed up and it was raining and so I caught the 10.05hrs train for Oudtshoorn. The other two stayed until the afternoon. The train ran via George and the same pass as I had crossed. yesterday by car but, instead of taking about two hours it took six to reach Oudtshoorn. When I got back I found that I should have got a pass to be out at night, but as it was only Saturday that I arrived it was OK. I spent the evening writing letters home and was in bed by half past eight to make up for last night.

Monday December 22nd 1941: Up at 04.30hrs this morning and after a cup of tea with bread and jam we began lectures. We spent most of the time being shown how to use a parachute, and this was before breakfast! At mid-day we were free for the rest of the day, so after lunch we went for a walk round the town. On the way, I posted the letters written last night.

Tuesday December 23rd 1941: Oudtshoorn. Navigation, First Aid and Photography were the lessons today and I quite enjoyed them. We went to the Toc H in Oudtshoorn this afternoon to pass the time away playing games. I stayed in camp during the evening playing snooker. I wrote letters home before going to bed.

Wednesday December 24th 1941: Oudtshoorn. I went up on my first official flight since I joined the RAF. It lasted one hour and twenty minutes. From the height of 8,000 feet I could see over the range of mountains laying to the south and into the sea between George and Mossel Bay. When we landed we were told that we had holidays for Christmas until Monday morning and that arrangements had been made for us to spend it in Mossel Bay. At first I was not too keen, but as the others wanted to go I went also. When we arrived at Mossel Bay we found that we are quartered in the Church Hall and had breakfast at a restaurant on the seashore, all free, which is just as well, as at the moment I have little money.

Thursday December 25th 1941: Mossel Bay. Christmas day and God bless all at home and may they enjoy this day. We were all up early and walked down to the restaurant in hot sunshine. After breakfast the three of us, Don, Doug and myself were sitting on a wall at the port when I saw that a boy was standing by the Cape Recieff lighthouse, semaphoring to another boy at the bottom of the cliff. Being an ex boy-scout I joined in and soon they replied to me. After a time they asked us up to the lighthouse for tea, for which we thanked them. Then came dinner with roast goose, sweet potatoes and vegetables, followed by hot Christmas pudding, all while the hot sun shone down on us! In the afternoon we went swimming in the Port, which I enjoyed very much.

While we were in the water the children from the lighthouse came down and introduced themselves to us. There are three boys and a girl called Marie. She is only fourteen, but later on the boys brought another of their sisters to see us. Her name is Jean and she is about nineteen. Don has fallen for her, I think. At tea time we all went to the lighthouse and met Mr and Mrs McLean, the children's father and mother. They are very nice people and made us very welcome. After tea Doug left us as he has a date in the dorp. Mr McLean took us over the lighthouse and showed us how it worked, as darkness had now fallen. It was quite late when we left, but promised meet the children again tomorrow.

Friday December 26th 1941: Mossel Bay. Went swimming again this morning and found the water very warm and clear. The pool we swim in is shark-free, for it is surrounded by rocks forming a large pool and six or seven smaller ones. It is possible to swim from one pool to another. Fish abound in the water and some are over a foot long. Two or three times I have felt their cold skin touch me while I have been in the water. On the sand at the bottom of the pools I have seen crayfish and small crabs. Shellfish and starfish are found on the rocks while under them octopi, about a foot or two long, hide. They are quite harmless and the fishermen use them for bait.

During the afternoon, I saw a five foot shark caught by rod and line. Don made arrangements to take Jean to a dance so I went to the films with Marie, promising her mother that as soon as the show was over we would walk down to the dance hall and meet the other two. The film was called 'City for Conquest', but was not much good. We did as Mrs McLean asked us to and after waiting a time, Jean and Don joined us. Together we walked to Cape St Blazie lighthouse and said 'Goodnight'.

Note: See date 25/12/41. The name of the lighthouse is St. Blaize not Recieff, which is at Port Elizabeth.

Saturday December 27th 1941: Mossel Bay. Spent this morning on the sands until lunchtime. In the afternoon we went, with all the children, to the Lyric bioscope to see the film 'The Prince and the Pauper'. It was very good, but childish. In the evening we went for a walk along the beach under the tropical moon and listened to the sea as it swept along the sands.

Sunday December 28th 1941: Mossel Bay. As this is the last day of our Christmas holiday, Mrs McLean asked Don and myself up to the lighthouse for lunch. In the afternoon we walked to the Tunnel Cave which runs under the cliffs to the rocks on the seashore. Then we returned for tea. At seven we said 'Goodbye' in the square as we left in the lorry on our long return journey. Mrs McLean has asked us over again next weekend if we can leave camp.

Monday December 29th 1941: Oudtshoorn. When I woke this morning I felt a little tired but I soon got over it. Meteorology and navigation were the lessons for today. Four letters arrived for me today. Three from home and one from Johannesburg. I replied in the evening. During the afternoon we got our maps ready for the flight tomorrow. I took a bath before going to bed.

On 'obliques'. Aerial photography exercise from an Avro Anson.

Letter dated 29th December 1941
from LAC L. Harris at Oudtshoorn SA

Darling wife of mine,

*Thank God mail arrived from England only a short while
ago. You can well imagine my joy to hear from you. I had
only just landed as we took off at 5.30am and I was
climbing out of the cockpit when a mechanic handed me
four letters. I could not wait, my sweet, until I took off my
parachute harness, but just sat down on the tail plane
and read them through. One of them was from Mother
and she wrote that she had heard from you so probably
she has answered your letter by now. One came from
Squibb, the other fellow from Alverstone, if you remember
him. He is now at a small place near York. The last was
from the Railway people asking me to fill up another form
about my pay. I was so happy to read of the antics of baby
Noel and do so look forward to playing with him.*

*I always blow you a kiss before I go to bed each night,
which is at about nine o'clock as we get up at 04.30 and
begin flying at 0530. It becomes so hot after midday that
all we do is lie on our beds and sweat. I am sitting on my
box writing to you clad only in shorts, but still sweat is
running from me. Outside the sun is as hot as hell for we
are in a valley and the rocks reflect the heat of the sun. I
should like a little English winter here for in our
bungalow in camp now it is like an oven, and rain would
be most welcome.*

*I wish you and Noel were out here with me for then Baby
could have all the oranges he wanted. I hope the foe has
not been over lately, but has given you quiet nights at
home. I do so hope you had a very happy Christmas and
that you enjoyed yourself. I did not enjoy it so much as I
would have had I been home, but it was not so bad. The
people at the Toc H arranged for about 30 of us to go over
to Mossel Bay, and it only cost us four shillings for petrol.*

*This time we went via Robinson Pass, which is not so high
as the Montagu Pass, but is even lovelier. When we arrived
in the seaside town we found beds ready for us in the
Church Hall and that we were to have our meals free at
one of the cafes near the seashore. On Christmas day I
went for a swim in a natural pool on the seashore for no
one swims in the open sea because of sharks.*

*We watched same fellows fishing from the rocks. They
used small octupus, called sea-cats, for bait. They catch
them with a pole with a hook on the end, and cut them
into pieces. While we watched they caught two "Mussel
brushes" weighing about fifteen pounds each. Then one
fellow hooked and landed a small shark about four feet
long. I was told it could bite off a hand or foot and even
kill a small child. Next day we went over Cape St. Blaize
lighthouse and enjoyed seeing how it worked.*

*On Sunday night we returned, fit again for our training.
We do a lot of flying from Oudtshoorn but just you look at
a map and see all the mountains. The Groot Zwartberg
Range, Roodebergen, Gamka Hill and the Kamnasie
Mountains, only to mention a few. With the Attoquas and
Outeniquas to the south, they look beautiful in the
morning light but, when the clouds are low, flying is not
so good.*

*Time to close, as I have to get my maps ready for flying
tomorrow as I am off again at half past five to
Windheuval Poort.*

All my love to you Sweetheart, your husband, Leslie.

Letter dated January 6th 1942.

My Own Darling Wife,

I received three letters and a cable from you yesterday. I was so happy to read of the doings of our little Noel. God grant that I will soon be back an England.

Please forgave me for only writing once or twice a week, but I am very busy these days getting through this course. If all goes well now I shall finish my training in this country in about 18 more weeks and so, some time in May I will be on my way to England and all I love.

I am so glad a letter of mine has reached you safely, and I hope by now many more have done so. I expect you get two or three at a time as I do. Thank you for saving the envelopes for my collection. I hope you enjoyed Christmas and may you have a happy birthday on the 14th January. I do so wish I could be home with you. There is little news here as I have only my work to occupy me, and that I must not write about just an case this letter should be captured by the foe during its journey home.

It is about eight in the evening so I will close now as it is time for me to go to bed as I take off at dawn tomorrow.

All my love, Leslie.

Letter dated Sunday 11th January 1942
from No. 45 Air School S.A.

Dearest Sweetheart,

I have been very busy ever since I arrived here. I have been flying every day this week and I am quite thankful for this day of rest. You must want to know what it is like to be an Observer over here so I will try (after much thought) to describe to you a flight from Oudtshoorn. To begin. I must warn you that the life of a navigator is by no means a bed of roses. The day before a long flight I am handed my route orders and details of which aircraft I am to fly in. The evening is spent working on my maps, plotting the best tracks and making notes of places to look for to make sure the aircraft is flying the way you want it to, for the flight is to be a dawn patrol leaving at 5.30am. Then I retire to my lonely bed to spend a restless night dreading the ordeal of the morrow.

Prompt at 3.30a.m. the next morning someone shakes me until I am half awake. So far I have never found out who he is because by the time I come to my senses he has gone. It then takes me about half an hour to climb out of bed. Over I stagger, still in my pyjamas, to get washed and to make an attempt to shave. Then I slip over to the mess for a cup of hot tea with bread and jam, if I can find any. That makes me feel much better and I then dress in my flying kit for it is quite cold up aloft in the early morning. It is by now about half past four and still dark, but I get over to the crew room to get my maps which I left there last night and check things out with the other boys who are flying in the other planes.

The mechanics are now wheeling the aircraft out of the hangers and warming up the engines so I hurry over to the Parachute Store to get my chute and harness but, to my disgust, no one has arrived yet. Off I hurry to the Meteorological Office to get the weather report, only to

1335461 L.A.C. L.HARRIS [AIR OBSERVER]
Course 15 A,
N°45 Air School,
Royal Air Force.
Oudtshoorn.
Cape Province.
South Africa.

Sunday January 11th 1942.

Dearest Sweetheart,

All my love to you, and our darling Baby, bless and keep you both safe for ever. Oh! Sweet love, I do so miss you and won't it be heaven to sleep together again. I pray each day that soon we will be reunited in happiness and peace. My love for you is too much to interpretate in words, but even if we are half the world apart I know you must feel our love close to each other even as I do. My darling Wife, no woman in the world is as sweet as you.

I have been very busy ever since I arrived here, I have been flying every day this week, and am quite thankful for this day of rest. You must want to know what it is like to be an observer out here so I will try [after much thought] to describe to you a flight from Oudtshoorn.

To begin I must warn you that the life of a navigator is by no means a bed of roses.

The day before a long flight I am handed my route, orders, and what 'plane I am to fly in. The evening is spent working working on my maps, plotting the best tracks, and making notes of places to look for to make sure the aircraft is flying the way you want it to, for the flight is to be a dawn patrol leaving at 5.30 A.M. Then I retire

*find that the Met Officer has overslept and has not got the
wind velocity yet, so I have to take what information he
has and hope to work out the wind speed in the air. Back I
rush to the Parachute Store and get my chute when I
suddenly find that I have left a glove on my bed so back I
run to my bungalow and dash out again at full speed to
the landing field. It is now ten past five so I try to find
plane AB which I am to navigate this morning but, after
twice checking the line of waiting aircraft, I am unable to
find it.*

*I shout to a flight mechanic "Where the Hell is AB?" only
to be told that it was stripped down last night for an
overhaul and that he does not know what other plane has
been assigned to me. Off I dash to the crew room again
and search frantically through the lists until at last I find
that CD is to be mine this flight. By now aircraft are
beginning to take off, so I run like the wind over to CD
and climb awkwardly into the cabin clinging on for dear
life to my instruments which the slip stream from the
engines is trying to fling over the aerodrome. Imagine, if
you can, my anger to find only the Radio Operator is at
his seat and he wants to know if I have seen the pilot! I
condemn them both to the hottest pit and yell to a
mechanic to go and find him.*

*After ten minutes the pilot arrives saying that he is sorry
that he kept us waiting, but gives no explanation why, so I
guess he had a thick night yesterday. At last we are
airborne and setting course on the first run. I am in the
middle of a tricky calculation to find the wind velocity
when the Radio Operator hands me a note radioed from
base asking my position. I use some very bad language
and put my finger on the place on the map I hope we are
and make out a chit for him to send back. Five minutes
later back comes the reply asking for me to report our
position every half hour. This I do.*

After altering course, having reached the first turning point, the pilot tells me that he will have to climb higher because of clouds. This means that I must begin my calculations all over again, which does not please me. I get lost for half an our or so, but I do not tell anyone until I see where I am and give the pilot the course for home. I almost cheer with joy when I see the base once more and, after landing, gladly climb out of the plane, stiff and hungry. Off I stagger to the crew room and fling my reports and log books at the Duty Officer. He has the cheek to hope that I have had a pleasant flip!

Just as life is beginning to look a little better the Met Officer comes across to me and asks me if I took any meteorological observations. My reply turns the air blue around him and he departs, turning as red as a boiled lobster. After a good breakfast I feel a new man and I am happy once again.

Of course I am only swinging the lead when I write all this, for it really is fine fun and I enjoy every minute of it. It is time to rest before the next days flight so, darling, good night

Your loving husband Leslie.

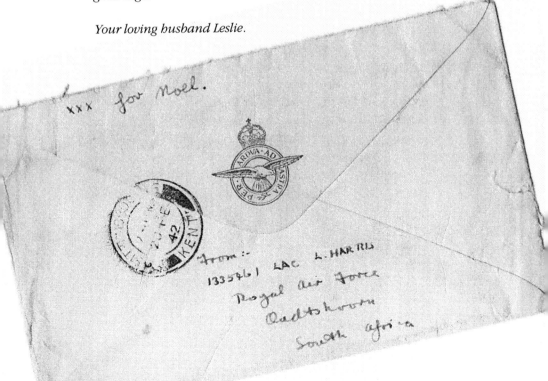

Letter dated January 15th 1942
from No.45 Air School, SA.

My Sweetest Darling,

The English mail arrived here at lunchtime and there
were two letters from you dated October 24th and
November 18th 1941, by the postmark. I was so happy to
read of England, my home, and those for whom I fly in
this hellish spot. Many happy returns for your birthday
and may we spend very many more together in more
peaceful days. I was going to send you a little gift but I
was advised. by the Padre not to risk anything in the Post
as, even if it arrived safely, you would probably have to
pay duty on it. Everything is quite good here, except the
heat, which is indescribable. We just lie on our beds from
noon. until about five as it is too hot even to move. I was
very surprised to hear how the Railway people are
behaving about my pay. I should be due for a rise from
the Railway on my next birthday. Let me know if any
thing more takes place. It is a pity that my old Station
Manager is not at Sittingbourne, for he would make
things alright until I get back home. The extra three
shillings and sixpence a week on the RAF pay is for an
extra allowance I made before leaving West Kirby. There
is little to tell about my work here. We just fly, fly and fly,
morning, noon and, before long, night as well. By the
way, I have been given the nickname of 'Blankey' which is
an Afrikanns word meaning something tiny I think. I
have just been reading pieces of your letters to the boys, as
we always do on letter day. Frank wrote, in his last letter
to his sweetheart, that he wanted to marry her when he
gets home to England. Well, he received a cable today
saying 'Yes' – so he wants all six in this room to celebrate
his engagement tonight.

Please forgive the bad hand writing, but I am writing this
last bit of the letter in the plane so I can post it as soon as I
land. We are just passing over the last range of mountains

*before arriving at Oudtshoorn and the air is a little
bumpy before coming in to land. I have just been thinking
about letters and their contents. Love letters, sad letters,
good letters. war letters, death letters, each in its own time
to tell its own story. No wonder I collect the stamps they
carry on their face. What could the stamps in my albums
tell if only they could speak?*

All my love, Your husband Leslie

January 16th 1942: *A Fallen Eagle. Avro Anson PM crashed near to
Willowmore as a result of a stall turn to avoid a high mountain peak.
The crew of four were killed as the aircraft caught fire on impact with
the ground. The pilot was South African, but the radio operator and
two cadets were English.*

Letter dated January 20th 1942
from No.45 Air School SA.

My own beloved wife,

*Another of your welcome letters arrived today and I was
so happy to hear from you again. I am slowly learning to
be able to navigate an aircraft with some degree of
accuracy.*

*On Saturday I was first Navigator and had to take a
plane about 200 miles along the coast and then out to sea
and from there I had to give the pilot a course to fly to get
back to base.*

*We arrived only three miles to the North of the aerodrome,
which is not too bad. Today we flew more than 300 miles
over the mountains and the Karoo desert to a very small
dorp of only six houses and, from there, to a road
junction miles from anywhere. We then set course for the
aerodrome and arrived only five miles east of
Oudtshoorn.*

*Sweetheart, I will close now, but will write again over the
weekend if all goes well.*

Your loving husband, Leslie.

Letter dated Saturday January 31st 1942
from No.45 Air School SA

My own darling wife,

*At last I have a moments peace in which to write to you.
We have been so busy these last ten days with the
mid-term exams, but, thank goodness, they are over at
last.*

*Everyone is hard at it and tomorrow morning, Sunday,
we are flying again to get as much time in the air as
possible. There is really little news, for, beyond my work, I
have very little to interest me.*

*Six of us went to the films this afternoon to see the picture
'Lady Eve', and enjoyed it no end.*

*This is about the only recreation we have in this dead
hole. I am so looking forward to being at home with you.*

Your loving husband, Leslie.

Letter dated Sunday February 8th 1942
from No.45 Air School SA

My own darling Monica,

*Your letter of December 18th arrived yesterday so, as I
have just been to Church parade, I will reply now. Dear
wife, if I should die in battle, teach Noel not to hate the foe
because they fight for their country and their loved ones
even as I do. Teach that more victories are won in peace
than ever on the field of war, but, if battle comes, send
him to the fore.*

*None of my kin shall stay back when brave men die. Tell
him he is a warrior of a family who's every generation has
given its blood for the cause it believed in. Sometimes in
the right, often in the wrong, but always true to its cause,
and never defeated, though often flung from the islands
they always fought their way back.*

*They died at Banockburn, at Flodden Field, at the last
stand of Montague in the Spanish Wars, in France, in
Germany, in the bloody War of the Roses in the Civil War,
in every clime, in every country they fought and died, but
were victorious.*

*Teach him to love a girl as sweet as you, tell him to
honour her above all things and to remember me.*

*But end all this and write of happier things yet to come. I
have rather a queer happening to tell you. On Wednesday
I was walking back to camp when I saw a native cart
which was upset in the ditch and, as it had been carrying
water melons, they were all over the road.*

*Of course I stopped to help pick them up and the two
native owners were quite pleased though they did not say
a word but both gave funny little bows when I left. The
queer part was that, as I came out of the camp gates
yesterday afternoon the elder native was there and he put*

in to my arms a carved wooden snake made from a root of a tree. Then, with another little bow, he turned and went away.

The guard on the gate told me that the native had been sitting on the ground for about five hours before I came out. Queer isn't it? I will bring it with me when I return to England. Well, my darling, I must close now.

Your loving husband, Leslie.

❖   ❖   ❖

The carved wooden snake referred to in the letter.

Letter dated Sunday February 15th 1942
from No. 45 Air School SA

Sweetheart,

Your very welcome cable arrived yesterday afternoon and I am happy to know that my letters have been received. The news from here is not very much.

We work all the week but, if ever I manage to get a week end off I go over to Mossel Bay for a swim. I stay with the lighthouse keeper of St Blaize light and a jolly Scotsman he is. I hope that one day we three get a chance of visiting Africa and I can introduce you to the friends I have made among the people of this land.

The English speaking people are jolly good to us, but the Afrikaans hate us like poison and we never risk going out after dark alone.

It does not do to write too much about the politics of South Africa, but I will have a lot to tell you when next we meet.

While I have been in Africa I have taken quite a number of photographs and have mounted then an album so we will have a good time looking through it and I can tell you all the tales about them.

Your loving husband, Leslie.

Letter dated Dawn of Tuesday February 17th 1942
Airborne en route for Cape Town.

My own dear wife,

Please excuse this letter being written in pencil but, as I am flying 9000 feet above sea level it is impossible to use a fountain pen due to lack of air pressure. Dawn is just breaking over in the East and we are well on our way to Cape Town.

It is great fun flying down to the Cape and I will post this letter to you when we arrive. It is a pity, but we will only have a short time to see the city and I will tell you about it in a following letter. I received a cable from you yesterday and I will reply to it on pay day.

I must close this short letter now as I must navigate all the way if we are to arrive safely.

God Bless you both. Leslie

P.S. Please excuse the bad writing but the aircraft is bumping about all over the sky.

Letter dated Thursday February 19th 1942 *from
No.45 Air School.*

My darling wife,

*Once more I am writing one of my short letters to let you
known how things are. I received a letter yesterday dated
the 12th of December and yet, about a week ago, I got one
dated the 18th of December, but I was glad to get it.*

*On Tuesday I flew down to Cape Town and had a nice
trip. On the way I wrote a short letter to you, which I
posted when we landed.*

*We only had two hours to see a little of the city so we
viewed very little, but I hope to see it again before I leave
this country. It would be grand if we can take a holiday
here after the war and see it all together.*

*I went on a photographic flight this morning and have
only just landed so I am writing this while waiting for
lunch.*

*There is a rumour that some more English mail has
arrived so I hope to get a letter from you today, so I expect
I will write again today or tomorrow.*

All my love. Your lover and husband Leslie.

Letter dated Monday February 23rd 1942
from No-45 Air School.

My own darling wife,

I am very happy as today is my birthday and the mail arrived at lunch time bringing three letters from you and one from mother. They are ones written on the 4th, 28th and 31st of December, so they were written before the one I got a day or so ago, dated the 5th of January 1942.

I am glad you were not lonely over Christmas, and baby Noel was a lucky boy to get so many birthday and Christmas gifts. Let us hope that next year we will be together and have a very jolly little party with a Christmas tree for Baby and jellies.

In mother's letter she says she misses Noel quite a lot and hopes he is alright and that she will see him again soon.

Do you mind if I close this short letter until tomorrow as six of us are going to have tea in town before going to the films.

All my love

Your loving husband Leslie

Letter dated Tuesday February 24th 1942
from No.45 Air School.

Dearest wife,

*All my love to you and our darling Noel, and I trust in
God to protect you for always. I doubt if I will have time to
finish this letter before tomorrow because I am taking off
for night flying at half past eight and it is after 7.30pm
now. If so I will finish it tomorrow.*

*As I wrote in my letter of yesterday, we went to see the film
'The Mummy's Hand' last night. I enjoyed it as it was a
ghostly picture of a mummy being brought to life and the
usual murders and mayhem. It was about eleven before
we got to bed. This is as late as I have been up for quite
some time. I am pleased you received the book I sent from
Durban.*

*I wondered if you would get it as I did not have time to
post it myself, so I asked the people in the shop I brought it
from to do so. Must close now as the engines are being
warmed up. Last night we flew to Calitzdorp and, though
it was a bit of a job navigating by the stars alone, I
managed to take the aircraft there and back safely. It was
very uneventful so I cannot write any more about it.*

*It is a little cooler today, thank goodness, and for once I
am not asleep in the afternoon. Most of the boys are
writing home, but there is not much news.*

*One day this week we hope to fly up to Bloemfontein in
the Orange Free State but of course it depends a lot on the
weather. It should be a good trip, as the country we should
fly over is quite picturesque.*

*On Sunday afternoon four of us went to the Congo Caves
which are about twenty miles from Oudtshoorn. They are
not as fine as those at Cheddar Gorge but we enjoyed
climbing through some parts which are not seen by most*

visitors and the result was we were in a mess by the time
we came out. We got a lift there and back by one of our
Officers and his wife, so we did not have to walk there, as
you might have thought.

Well my love, I must close now to get on with my work.

God Bless you both, Leslie.

❖　❖　❖

On 18th February 1942, LAC Harris flew down to Cape Town in Avro
Anson PN. After only two hours in the city he returned to Oudtshoorn.

Letter dated Saturday March 7th 1942
from Toc H, Oudtshoorn.

My darling wife,

Just a short note to let you know that I am OK. I received your two telegrams yesterday. You are a dear to remember me on my birthday. I have just been shopping for one or two odds and ends and have just come in to the TOC H for dinner before going to the films, and, as paper and ink is handy I thought I would drop you a line.

All my love to you and baby Noel and please God I will be home in a few weeks now. If all goes well I should finish Navigation School within a week or so and then I will only have bombing and gunnery to do before I finish. It is reported that some more English mail is in and so I hope to get some letters front you on Monday.

Everything is much the same here but it is getting a little cooler now that winter has arrived. While flying this morning I had to wear gloves for the first time in this country. As it is nearly six o'clock and I want to listen to the news from home I will close for now but will write a longer letter tomorrow, if all goes well.

All my love, Leslie.

Letter dated Sunday March 8th 1942
from No.45 Air School

My Sweet wife,

Today, being Sunday, I was up late. There is little news today as I have not been out of camp, being too lazy to dress and, anyway, there is nowhere to go. Instead I have done a little studying and have put some more snaps in my album.

I am enclosing a snap that Don took of me as I was checking my maps before a flight. I did not know that he was taking it so hence the peculiar stance.

As you see, we do not wear full flying kit as it is too hot, but I have my parachute harness on. There is little news in this dump as we are cut off from all the news. The war seems in another world.

Good night my darling.

Your loving husband, Leslie.

Letter dated Sunday March 18th 1942
from No.45 Air School.

My own darling wife,

Two letters arrived from you yesterday, dated the 18th and 25th of January. I am so very happy whenever I have letters from you. This past week we have been hard at work with our final navigation exams which, I am glad to say, all the course passed. If all goes well, I have only three weeks bombing and three more weeks at gunnery before I get my wings. Then, please God, I will soon be on my way home.

Noel must look nice in his suit, but I do not like grey very much as a colour, but I suppose wool is scarce in England now. I intend to bring one or two odds and ends home with me, if all goes well. I am out in the sun a lot so I am getting brown, but as all the boys are also, we do not notice it.

I had a letter from Mother the same time as yours and she gave me all the news from the Island. I went playing bowls for the first time yesterday afternoon. I had a lot of fun, even if I was not very successful in the game.

Today, being Sunday, everyone is either in bed asleep or writing home as I am. We make a rule of writing each Sunday before we go out. Frank Sayles is trying to write to his best girl in England and is having a job to do so, as every one is telling him what to say.

He was twenty on Friday so we celebrated his birthday and our passing out exams at the same time. I will close now.

Your lover and husband, Leslie.

Letter dated March 22nd 1942

from No. 45 Air School

My Darling Wife,

I received your sweet letter dated the 10th of January and I was happy to hear from you, my love. Today, being Sunday, I am being very lazy as usual and doing nothing but sleep and read. We are leaving Oudtshoorn in a few days, if all goes well, for the gunnery school so, please God, I will soon be on my way home. I am longing to see all my loved ones again.

We have been bombing these past few days, but are still not much good at it. You begin to understand war when you load up with bombs, even if they are small practice ones. As I press the bomb release button and the bombs go sailing earthwards it sends a queer feeling over my whole body, like a hand of death covering my eyes and the cold breath of the long dead moves my hands over the control switches. I have not been out of camp much this week.

We went to the pictures on Wednesday to see the film 'Ninochca'. I remembered when we saw it together when I was courting you, my darling. As I only wrote to you yesterday I can think of no more to write, so I will close.

Your loving husband, Leslie.

Letter dated March 26th 1942 *from No.45 Air School.*

My beloved wife,

I have only five more weeks of training before returning to England. We have our bombing exams next week, so I will not have time to write as I have a lot of swotting to do before then. I have got some pairs of stockings for you which I was going to post, but as some duty may be payable so I have decided to pack them in my kit instead. How is our little Noel? I hope that he will remember me when I come home. I have enclosed a ticket for our Passing Out Dance, of course, it is beyond all dreams that you could be here but, to me, you will always be near me wherever I am. There is a dinner between our course and one or two of our Officers before the dance, which I will attend, but I doubt if I will go to the dance as you know, I dislike them. All the boys are inviting a girl, that is why the cards were printed, but mine is only for you.

Your lover and husband, Leslie.

No 10 OTU, St Eval 1943: *Sgt Leslie Harris and the crew of Whitley Mk VI BD260 'N'. This aircraft attacked a U-boat on 12th March 1943.*

Letter dated Tuesday April 7th 1942
from No.43 Air School, Port Alfred.

My own darling wife,

*All my love to both my dear ones and God keep you all
well and happy for ever. As you see by the new address, I
have left Oudtshoorn and moved some little distance
Northward and to the coast. But to begin at the
beginning… Last Wednesday we had our bombing exam
which I am glad to say, everyone passed. In the evening
we held our Dinner and Dance which was a great success
and all had a good time. I went to the dance to help out
with the refreshments, but got fed up so returned to camp
early. I spent most of Thursday saying 'goodbye' to the
friends I have made during my stay in Oudtshoorn, and
the rest of the time I was busy packing. We left
Oudtshoorn in the afternoon on Friday and arrived at
Port Elizabeth about ten the following day. As the train
onwards to Port Alfred did not leave until 23.25hrs, we
had the day to ourselves. I rang up my old friend the
Lighthouse Keeper, who, I believe I told you, was
transferred from Mossel Bay to Port Elizabeth a month or
so ago. He was pleased I could stay a few hours and came
down in his car to meet me at the station. Before I could
go to Cape Recieffe Lighthouse we had to get a permit from
the Harbourmaster, but with my being in uniform, it was
granted. I saw all over the Lighthouse and went for a
swim and helped to catch fish for our tea. I was very sorry
to say goodbye as the train left the station.*

*We arrived at Port Alfred at lunchtime and went at once
to the camp. It is not too bad, the food is well cooked and
the coffee is better than at Oudtshoorn. After tea we took a
walk round the town, it is very small but, as we are only
here three weeks, we do not mind at all.*

Good night and God bless you, my only love, Leslie

There is a gap in the correspondence from the 8th of April 1942 up to the 30th October 1942. Information from Log Books and researched sources has been used to complete the story as far as possible. The Air Gunnery Course at Number 43 Air School Port Alfred continued until the 24th of April 1942. Ground training was given before live air firing exercises were carried out. Airspeed Oxford aircraft, fitted with a mid-upper turret carrying either a gas-operated drum-fed Vickers gun or a Lewis machine gun were used. After flying four hours and ten minutes and having achieved a 79% pass, Leslie, together with his other Course members, departed South Africa by sea, after being awarded their half brevet as Observers and promotion to Sergeant.

The troop ship *Leopoldville* left Cape Town on the 30th of April 1942 and apparently arrived in Great Britain unscathed. On the 24th of June 1942 Leslie commenced further training in navigation at Penhros in Wales, attending No.26 Course and flying in Avro Ansons and Bristol Blenheim Mk. IV aircraft. By the 27th of July 1942 he had successfully completed the course and was posted to ' C' Flight of No.24 Operational Training Unit, commencing training on the 15th of August 1942, again in the faithful "Annie" Anson,, flying from RAF Honeybourne. This stage of training finished on the 29th of August 1942.

Transferring to 'C' Flight of No.24 OTU on the 7th of September 1942, Leslie flew in Armstrong Whitworth 'Whitley' Mk. V twin-engined bombers. This part of training concentrated on cross-country flying both by day and night and included high level bombing and air-to-air gunnery practice to simulate, as far as possible, wartime flying conditions. Sixteen of these practice sorties were flown, the course finishing on the 25th of September 1942. On the 14th of August 1942, a detachment of No.10 Operational Training Unit had been set up at RAF St. Eval in Cornwall, flying Whitley Mk V aircraft. They operated there until the 19th of July 1943. The purpose of this detachment was to give support to the aircraft of Coastal Command who were engaged in what became known as 'The Battle of the Atlantic' – the destruction of U-boats that were attacking, unfortunately with great success, Allied convoys sailing to and from the UK.

Sergeant L. Harris was posted. to St. Eval in October 1942 and was soon taking part in 'Operational Sweeps' as the sorties were known. On the 20th of October his aircraft had to return from such a sweep with the port engine exhaust broken. On the 24th of October one engine broke down, necessitating a return to the comparative safety of base.

On the 27th of October 1942, whilst returning from an Operational Sweep, Whitley '0', airframe No. Z6959, suffered an engine failure and fire and crashed one mile East of St Erne, Cornwall. Sergeant Harris , with the rest of the crew, were fortunate in being able to bale out of the doomed aircraft. They owed their lives to the courageous action of their pilot, Sergeant Vic Howarth, who stayed at the controls. Sergeant Harris, and, presumably, the rest of the crew, were able to claim membership of the 'Caterpillar Club', founded by the Irvin Air Chute Company, for airmen who had saved their lives by using a parachute provided by that Company. On landing heavily Sergeant Harris found that he had fractured an ankle and was sent to the Atlantic Hospital, Newquay, Cornwall, to recover.

Having been separated from his crew, Sergeant Harris was next posted to No. 24 Operational Training Unit at Long Marston. Flying again in Whitley Mk V aircraft he flew eight sorties between January 26th 1943 and February 7th 1943. Six of these sorties were carried out at night and involved high level bombing and cross country navigation.

Whilst in 'E' Flight he met Sergeant Pilot E.C. Parritt and became the Observer in his crew.

*Letter dated **Friday October 30th 1942** from the*
Atlantic Hospital Newquay Cornwall.

Dearest Mother,

All my love and hope that you are OK. I am well as my ankle is only slightly fractured and I have not had to stay in bed at all and have, in fact, been wandering about the place and getting in everyone's way.

The doctor said this morning that I can leave next week but will have to keep the plaster on for about a month so I am looking forward to a longish leave this time. I am now a member of the Caterpillar Club having saved my life by jumping by parachute from a crashing aircraft. It is not as bad as it sounds.

It would be OK if poor Vic had not tried to land it in flames, because he was killed. All the rest got off OK without a scratch. This place is dull, but I have lots to read, and in a day or so, hope to be out again.

So until my next letter, all my love, Leslie.

Letter dated February 10th 1943 *from No.24*
Operational Training Unit, Honeybourne.

Dearest Mother,

In great haste. On leave from today until March the first.
Write soon to Ford End and tell me when you can get
some time off so I can come down to the Island.

Love Leslie

(Note: This was a Letter Card addressed to Mrs D. Harris, The
Fire Station, South Street, Newport, Isle of Wight. At this time
she was serving in the Auxiliary Fire Service. As with many women
of her time, she did her bit towards the war effort.)

Ladies of the Isle of Wight Auxillary Fire Service.

Following a return posting to 'A' Flight of No.10 OTU at St. Eval, Sergeant Harris, with Sergeant G.C. Parritt as his pilot, resumed anti-submarine patrols. These could be long and dangerous for the air crews involved. By the 19th of July 1943, when No. 10 detachment flew its last patrol, it had lost no less than 33 Whitleys, either to enemy action or engine failures far out at sea.

On the 12th of March 1943, Sergeant Harris was flying in Whitley 'N', airframe number BD260, when it suffered damage to its port wing during an attack on a U-Boat found on the surface that was determined to make a fight for its survival.

On the 22nd of March 1943, this time flying in Whitley 'A', airframe No. 26491, a further attack on a U-Boat was made. Unfortunately the result was inconclusive. Having flown ten sorties in twelve days at St. Eval the time to leave came soon enough.

The next posting was to 'B' Flight of No.1658 Heavy Conversion Unit at Riccall in Yorkshire for training on the four-engined Handley Page Halifax. Conversion Units tended to receive aircraft that had been withdrawn from front line squadrons and many of these unsung hero's (heroines?) were as battle weary as their former crews. Between the 21st April 1943 and 7th May 1943, Sergeant Harris flew nine sorties, carrying out various familiarisation exercises with the equipment installed in this particular type of aeroplane. This included the use of 'Gee', an electronic radio pulse system used by the Navigator to identify his position, which in turn assisted the Bomb-aimer to drop his bombs with greater accuracy. Two of the sorties were carried out with Sergeant Pilot G.C. Parritt, probably for crew familiarisation purposes.

Letter Card dated Sunday 20th June 1943 *from Sergeant's Mess, RAF Holme-on-Spalding Moor.*

Dearest Mother,

Got a little leave so hope to be able to get down onto the Island on Wednesday. I hope to come early and stay until Thursday morning. I shall be coming alone, so hope to see you soon. If you cannot get Wednesday afternoon off I will meet the train from Cowes at Sandown, if all goes well.

All my love, Your loving son, Leslie.

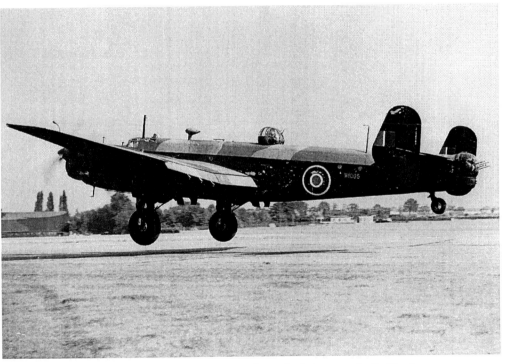

A Halifax B Mk II, similar to the aircraft in which Sergeant Leslie Harris would have carried out part of his further training in April 1943 at No.1658 Operational Training Unit, Riccall, Yorks.

Photo courtesy of the London Transport Museum.

Letter Card dated Sunday evening June 27th 1943
from the Sergeants Mess, RAF Holme-on-Spalding Moor.

Beloved Wife,

*Arrived OK, but had to walk 1½ miles from Goole, so did
not get to camp until nearly nine this morning. Spent the
time until about three in bed, so I did not do too bad. It is
now 8.30pm and Val and Ralph are still missing so we do
not expect then until tomorrow. Just a short note to let you
know that I am OK and to sent my love to you and Noel.*

Your loving husband, Leslie.

*Halifax air crews of No 76 Squadron have a last few minutes rest while
waiting for transport to take them to their aircraft. The station padre,
standing by the lorry, sees them off.*   Photo courtesy of the Imperial War Museum.

Telephone No. : { SPRINGWELL 2119
                 { GLOUCESTER }

Telegraphic Address :
  RECORDS TELEX, GLOUCESTER.

RECORD OFFICE,
  ROYAL AIR FORCE,
    GLOUCESTER.

Any communications on the
subject of this letter should
be addressed to :—

AIR OFFICER i/c RECORDS,
    Address as opposite,
and the following number
quoted :— A2M/1335461

Date 22 July 1943.

Your Ref. : ....

Madam,
        I have to inform you that your
husband No. 1335461 Sergeant Leslie HARRIS
was promoted to the rank of Flight Sergeant with effect from 1st May 1943.

                I am, Madam,
                Your obedient Servant,

                    for Air Commodore,
                Air Officer i/c Records,
                Royal   Air   Force.

Mrs. L. Harris,
25 Eastwood Road,
Kilton Regis,
SITTINGBOURNE.

May 25th 1943 saw the newly-promoted Flight Sergeant Harris commencing duty with No. 76 Squadron, then based at Linton-on-Ouse and equipped with the Merlin-engined and Dowty undercarriaged Halifax Mk V. Four further 'working up' flights were carried out between 30th May and 9th June.

On the 16th June 1943, No. 76 Squadron transferred to the aerodrome at Holme-upon-Spalding Moor.

On the evening of 28th June 1943, Halifax Mark V, Airframe No. DK137, code letters MP-R joined the rest of 76 Squadron's aircraft waiting for the signal to take off. The chosen target was the German city of Cologne. A total of 608 aircraft – including Halifaxes, Stirlings, Lancasters, Wellingtons and Mosquitoes – took off to deliver the heaviest raid yet carried out on that town during "The Battle of the Ruhr". The weather forecast had indicated that Cologne would be cloud covered, necessitating the dropping of sky markers by 'Oboe'-equipped Mosquitoes. Oboe was a target-locating system designed to assist the bombers. In spite of the cloud cover, the German anti-aircraft fire was extremely heavy and accurate, due to the use of radar prediction information supplied to the gunners to give them details of height and direction so that shells could be fused accordingly. Bombers also received the attention of batteries of searchlights, often being first picked out by a radar controlled light and then being 'coned' by the other lights in the battery. This usually meant a violent corkscrew manoeuvre by the pilot to avoid either gunfire or night-fighters.

Twenty-five aircraft were destroyed during the course of this particular raid, including two Halifaxes belonging to No.76 Squadron.

One of these was DK137 MP-R. It was shot down over Votten, North of Liege in Belgium. There were no survivors.

Halifax B Mk V aircraft of No 76 Squadron at Holme-upon-Spalding Moor line up ready for take-off. Sgt Harris and the crew of DK137 would have formed part of a similar line on 28th June 1943.

Photos courtesy of the Imperial War Museum.

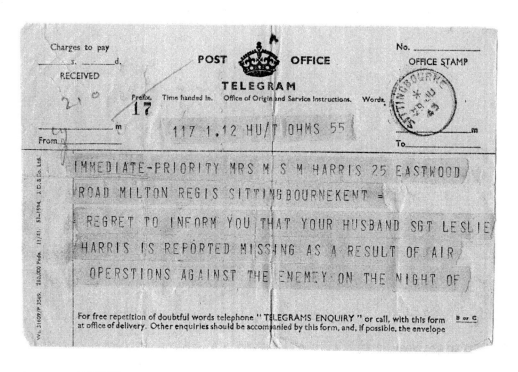

POST ✠ OFFICE

TELEGRAM

Charges to pay ___ s. ___ d.

RECEIVED 2 1 0

Prefix. Time handed In. Office of Origin and Service Instructions. Words.

17

From ___ m

117 1.12 HU/T OHMS 55

No. ___

OFFICE STAMP

To ___ m

IMMEDIATE-PRIORITY MRS M S M HARRIS 25 EASTWOOD ROAD MILTON REGIS SITTINGBOURNEKENT = REGRET TO INFORM YOU THAT YOUR HUSBAND SGT LESLIE HARRIS IS REPORTED MISSING AS A RESULT OF AIR OPERSTIONS AGAINST THE ENEMEY ON THE NIGHT OF

For free repetition of doubtful words telephone " TELEGRAMS ENQUIRY " or call, with this form at office of delivery. Other enquiries should be accompanied by this form, and, if possible, the envelope   B or C

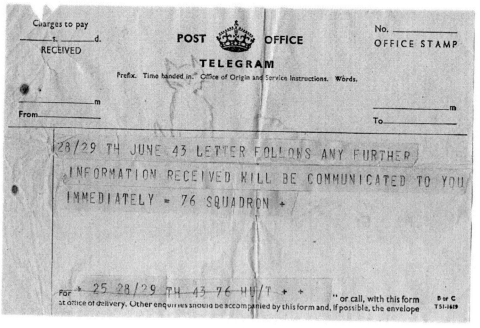

POST ✠ OFFICE

TELEGRAM

Charges to pay ___ s. ___ d.

RECEIVED

Prefix. Time handed In. Office of Origin and Service Instructions. Words.

From ___ m

No. ___

OFFICE STAMP

To ___ m

28/29 TH JUNE 43 LETTER FOLLOWS ANY FURTHER INFORMATION RECEIVED WILL BE COMMUNICATED TO YOU IMMEDIATELY = 76 SQUADRON +

For + 25 28/29 TH 43 76 HU/T + +

at office of delivery. Other enquiries should be accompanied by this form and, if possible, the envelope   " or call, with this form   B or C   T51-1619

76S/68/   /P.1.

No: 76 Squadron,
R.A.F. Station,
Holme on Spalding Moor.
Yorks.

June 29th. 1943.

Dear Mrs. Harris,

It was with the utmost regret that I had to telegraph you and tell you that your husband, Sgt. Leslie Harris, failed to return from an operational flight against the enemy last night.

He and his crew were detailed to attack the important, and consequently heavily defended, target of Cologne. At the moment I am afraid that I can do no more than tell you that according to statistics of past losses more men who are reported missing are prisoners-of-war than otherwise, and at the very worst his chances of being safe are at least fifty-fifty.

Prior to this, his first operational trip with the Squadron, your husband had completed 10 Coastal Sweeps. He had a very responsible job, and was rated very highly by his Captain. He was flying with a first rate crew, and I am confident that whatever it was that happened, they were able to deal with it.

If there is anything I can do to help you, I hope you will not hesitate to get in touch with me. The moment we hear any further news, I will immediately communicate with you, and in the meantime, please accept on behalf of myself and the entire Squadron, my sincerest sympathy in these anxious days of waiting.

Yours very sincerely,

D. C. SMITH.
Wing Commander, Commanding
No: 76 Squadron.   R. A. F.

Mrs. M.S.M. Harris,
25, Eastwood Road,
Milton Regis,
Sittingbourne.

The Royal Air Force Benevolent Fund.

PATRON: H.M. THE KING.

CHAIRMAN: THE RT. HON. LORD RIVERDALE, G.B.E.

Telephone No. : HOVE 3992.

All Communications to be addressed to the Secretary

EATON HOUSE.

14, EATON ROAD.

HOVE, SUSSEX.

Our Reference   MB/AMS/133.

5th July, 1943

Mrs. L.Harris,
        25 Eastwood Rd.,
            Kilton Regis,
                Sittingbourne,
                    Kent.

Dear Madam,

The Council of the Royal Air Force Benevolent Fund have learnt with much regret that your husband is reported missing, and I am asked to convey to you their very sincere sympathy.

I am to inform you that you should at the moment be in receipt of a temporary allowance from the Air Ministry, which will continue for 26 weeks pending further information concerning your husband.

If the allowance is not being received, you should communicate immediately with the Secretary, Air Ministry, (Accts 7) Dept.O.A., Redhill, Worcester.

Should you be in need of some temporary assistance either now or at any time in the future, please let me know and I will arrange for our Representative to interview you at the earliest opportunity.

In the meantime, if I can help or advise in any way perhaps you will kindly write to me, otherwise please do not trouble to answer this letter.

Yours truly,

Squadron Leader,
Joint Secretary.

Gerrard 9234

(Casualty Branch)
77, Oxford Street,

P 405791/2/43/P.4.A.2.   W.1.

12 July, 1943.

Madam,

I am commanded by the Air Council to express to you their great regret on learning that your husband, Sergeant Leslie Harris, Royal Air Force, is missing as the result of air operations on the night of 28/29th June, 1943, when a Halifax aircraft in which he was flying as navigator set out for action over enemy territory and failed to return.

This does not necessarily mean that he is killed or wounded, and if he is a prisoner of war he should be able to communicate with you in due course. Meanwhile enquiries are being made through the International Red Cross Committee and as soon as any definite news is received you will be at once informed.

If any information regarding your husband is received by you from any source you are requested to be kind enough to communicate it immediately to the Air Ministry.

The Air Council desire me to convey to you their sympathy in your present anxiety.

                              I am, Madam,
                                Your obedient Servant,

                                Charles Evans.

Mrs. L. Harris,
    25, Eastwood Road,
        Milton Regis,
            Sittingbourne,
                Kent.

TELEPHONE:
Gerrard 9234
~~HOLBORN 3434~~
Extn......3802....
Any communications on the
subject of this letter should
be addressed to :—
THE
UNDER SECRETARY
OF STATE.
and the following number
quoted:—
P. 405791/2/43/P.4.Cas/B.4.

AIR MINISTRY,
Casualty Branch
~~LONDON, W.C.2.~~
73-77 Oxford Street
London, W.1.

Your Ref. ....   30th September, 1943

~~Sir~~/Madam,

     I am directed to refer to the letter
dated 12th July, 1943,   notifying you
that your husband, Sergeant Leslie Harris,
Royal Air Force,
was reported missing on night of 28/29th
and to inform you that the following June,
information has been received through 1943
the International Red Cross Committee.

       "29/6 Halifax three dead
       Sergeant 1313333 Parritt
       two unknown."

Mrs. L. Harris,
25 Eastwood Road,
Milton Regis,
Sittingbourne,
Kent.

A.4381.   /T.4

As there were seven members in crew,

It is not possible on this information
to identify the unknown but as your husband
is still unaccounted for and the above were
members of his crew it is considered that
you would wish to be notified of this report.

I am to add an expression of the
Department's sympathy with you in your
anxiety and to assure you that you will be
notified of any further information received.

I am, Madam,
Your obedient Servant,

for Director of Personal Services.

A.4381.

TELEPHONE: GERRARD 9234

Extn.............

Any communications on the
subject of this letter should
be addressed to :—

THE SECRETARY,

and the following number
quoted :— P.405791/2/43/P.4.B.3.

Your Ref. ....

AIR MINISTRY

(Casualty Branch),

73-77, OXFORD STREET,

27ᵗʰ November, 1943. W.1.

Madam,

I am directed to refer to a letter from this Department dated the 30th September, 1943, and to inform you with regret that a report has now been received from the International Red Cross Committee which states that Sergeant Parritt and an unknown airman were buried on the 1st July at St. Trond, Belgium. The grave numbers are 201 and 202 respectively.

A further report states that two more unknown airmen belonging to this crew were buried at St. Trond in graves numbered 215 and 253.

It is greatly regretted that as there was a crew of seven, it is not possible to identify the unknown, but as your husband, Sergeant Leslie Harris, Royal Air Force, was a member of this crew, these reports are forwarded for your information.

I am to assure you that any further details received will be immediately forwarded to you and to again express the sincere sympathy of the Department with you in your anxiety.

I am, Madam,
Your obedient Servant,

J. G. Shreeve

for Director of Personal Services.

Mrs. L. Harris,
   25, Eastwood Road,
      Milton Regis,
         Sittingbourne,
            Kent.

Any communications on the
subject of this letter should
be addressed to :—
THE
UNDER SECRETARY
OF STATE,
and the following number
quoted :- P.405791/2/43/P.4.Cas.B.4.

Your Ref. ....

AIR MINISTRY

(Casualty Branch),

73-77, OXFORD STREET,

W.1.

9th December 1943.

Madam,

    I am directed to refer to your letter dated 30th November 1943, regarding your husband, No. 1335461 Sergeant L. Harris, Royal Air Force.

    I am to inform you that all Royal Air Force personnel should wear identity discs but the Department is sure you will appreciate in some instances due to the circumstances attending the catastrophe the means of identification become detached from the bodies of members of the crew.

    The German Authorities in their report correctly named the aircraft as a Halifax. Sergeant Parritt's correct name and service number were quoted and the reports link the "unknown" members of the crew with Sergeant Parritt, stating specifically that they were members of the same crew. The Department's experience of the German Authorities after four years is that all information at their disposal regarding our casualties is given to us and there is unfortunately no reason to doubt the accuracy of their reports in this instance.

    I am to assure you that enquiry will continue to be made from all possible sources and should any news of your husband be received it will be passed to you at once.

    In writing this, I am, once again, to add an expression of the sincere sympathy of the Department with you in your grave anxiety.

               I am, Madam,
                  Your obedient Servant,

Mrs. L. Harris,
25 Eastwood Road,
Milton Regis,
KENT.

            J. G. Shreeve

    for Director of Personal Services.

Gerrard 9234
xxxxxxxxxx

73-77 Oxford Street,

London, W.1.

P.405791/2/P.4.(b)

31st January, 1944

Madam,

    I am commanded by the Air Council to
state that in view of the lapse of time and
the absence of any further news regarding
your husband, 1335461 Sergeant L. Harris,
since the date on which he was reported
missing, they must regretfully conclude that
he has lost his life, and his death has now
been presumed, for official purposes, to
have occurred on the 29th June, 1943.

    The Council desire me to express again
their sympathy with you in the anxiety which
you have suffered, and in your bereavement.

        I am, Madam,
        Your obedient Servant,

Charles Evans

Mrs. L. Harris,
   25 Eastwood Road,
      Milton Regis,
         Sittingbourne,
           Kent.

AIR MINISTRY,

2, SEVILLE STREET,

LONDON, S.W.1.

P.40579/43/S.14.Cas.C.6.

26 November, 1947.

Dear Mrs. Harris,

Further to the Department's letter of 27th November, 1943, I now write to tell you the result of extensive investigations into the fate of men reported buried on the airfield at Brusthem, near St. Trond, which have been made by the Royal Air Force Missing Research and Enquiry Service in Belgium.

It was discovered that nine aircraft had crashed in Central Belgium on 29th June and 4th July, 1943, involving some fifty-two deaths and I regret to inform you that the enemy authorities were not only unable to identify the majorit of the fallen airmen but also neglected to make an accurate record of the burial positions. It was therefore necessary to conduct an exhumation of all the graves on the airfield and it was finally established that your husband was one of twenty-six airmen buried in twenty coffins whose remains, unfortunately, could not be identified.

Moreover, as the airfield was not suitable as a permanent cemetery, all the coffins were subsequently transferred to the British Military Cemetery at Heverle, near Louvain; the twentyOsix unidentified airmen being laid to rest in graves 1 - 20, row D, plot 6.

These graves have been registered collectively in their names and marked with temporary white crosses of standard design. In due course these will be replaced by permanent

Mrs. L. Harris,
    25, Eastwood Road,
        Milton Regis,
            Sittingbourne,
                Kent.

/headstones

headstones and the Imperial War Graves Commission will be
responsible in perpetuity for their proper care.

I regret that this information is of such a distressing
nature but I feel you would not wish us to withhold it.

Yours sincerely,

S Rowley.

TELEPHONE:

~~ABBEY 3411~~ Sloane 3467

Extn............

Any communications on the
subject of this letter should
be addressed to:—
THE UNDER SECRETARY
OF STATE, AIR MINISTRY,
and the following number
quoted:— P.405791/43/S.14.Cas.B2.

Your Ref...............

AIR MINISTRY,
2, Seville Street,
LONDON, S.W.1.

15ᵗʰ December, 1947.

Madam,

      I am directed to refer to your letter dated 30th October,
1947, and to say that the information obtained from German
sources during the war respecting your husband and his aircrew
companions was that his pilot, Sergeant Parritt, and three
unidentified members, had been laid to rest in graves 201, 202,
215 and 253, in the cemetery at St. Trond.

      The graves of the latter were exhumed by the Royal Air
Force Missing Research and Enquiry Service, but, unhappily, it
was apparent that the crash was a very severe one, and it was
not possible to establish individual identities from the remains
that were found. As mentioned in the Department's letter of
29th November, the remains of 23 other airmen who lost their
lives at about the same time were also unidentifiable, and
amongst these in graves whose numbers were never disclosed by the
German authorities and which could not be established from the
inaccurate records maintained by them, were those of the three
other members of your husband's crew.

      You will appreciate that, under the circumstances, the
Department was unable to arrange for an adequate collective
marking for the three members originally occupying graves 202,
215, and 253 at St. Trond, and the collective registration of all
20 unidentified graves had therefore to be effected.

                        I am, Madam,
                        Your obedient Servant,

Mrs. M. Harris,
    25, Eastwood Road,
      Milton Regis,
        Sittingbourne,
          Kent.

IMPERIAL WAR GRAVES COMMISSION,

WOOBURN HOUSE, WOOBURN GREEN,

HIGH WYCOMBE, BUCKS.

6 APR 1948

Dear Sir or Madam,

I venture to ask for your assistance in completing the attached form.

The Imperial War Graves Commission have been entrusted, for this war as for the last, with the duty of permanently commemorating those members of His Majesty's Naval, Military and Air Forces from all parts of the British Empire who die in the service of the Allied cause. The Commission will consequently be responsible for marking and caring for the graves, or, in the case of those who have no known grave, for making provision for other suitable form of commemoration and also for recording all names in permanent Registers. This work will be carried out at the cost of the Commission, whose funds are provided by all the Governments of the Empire.

A headstone of the same simple pattern will, as before, mark each grave ; thus every man, rich or poor, General or Private, will be honoured in the same way.

In order to carry out these duties, and to complete the permanent Registers, the Commission desire certain additional information which they hope you will be so good as to supply on the attached form, which should then be returned to the Commission.

You will notice that a space has been left on the form for a personal inscription to be selected by the relatives, if they so desire, for engraving on the headstone. Where, owing to the course of military operations, it has so far been impossible to find or identify a grave, no personal inscription should be inserted on the form. Should the grave eventually be discovered, I shall, of course, write to you again, and you will then have a further opportunity to choose an inscription.

Some relatives have expressed the wish to pay for this personal inscription, and an opportunity will be given to them later on of meeting the cost. Should they not wish to do so, the cost will be borne by the Commission.

Yours faithfully,

FABIAN WARE,

Vice-Chairman.

(5141/1729) Wt. P2901/2379 50m. 4/47 T. & B. Gp. 468.

HS

IMPERIAL WAR GRAVES COMMISSION,

WOOBURN HOUSE,

WOOBURN GREEN,

HIGH WYCOMBE,

BUCKS.

23.8.52.

Dear Madam,

The Commission are making steady progress with the permanent marking of war graves in many parts of the world, and the headstone engraved with the personal inscription chosen by you is amongst those already erected.

A number of relatives have expressed a wish to participate in the commemoration by contributing towards the cost of engraving the inscription of their choice. This cost has increased since the first letters were sent out and any sum up to £1. 0s. 0d. is now being accepted.

Should you wish to make a contribution it may be sent as soon as convenient, accompanied by the form below, in the envelope enclosed, which requires no postage stamp.

An official receipt will be sent for each contribution, and, if this does not reach you within fourteen days of the despatch of your remittance, the Commission should be informed.

Heverlee War Cemetary
Louvain Belgium.   Yours faithfully,

J. Higinson

SECRETARY.

Detach by tearing along the dotted line.

REMITTANCE FORM

In reply to your letter I enclose *Five shillings*
as a contribution to the cost of engraving the personal inscription chosen by me on the permanent headstone which has been erected by the Commission on the grave of

FLT. SGT. (NAV.) L. HARRIS.

1335461. R.A.F. VR, in HEVERLEE WAR CEM. LOUV

Signed *Monica Harris*

From :—

MRS. M. HARRIS,
25 EASTWOOD RD.,
MILTON REGIS,
SITTINGBOURNE,
KENT.

Cheques, postal and money orders should be crossed and mai

(42581) Wt.P.0468/2680 100,000 4/51 A.& E.W.Ltd. Gp.686

3050   **PERSONAL INSCRIPTION**

RECEIVED *with thanks*   £   s.   d.

from Mrs. M. Harris.   5 0

IMPERIAL WAR GRAVES COMMISSION,
WOOBURN GREEN, Bucks.

31st October 1952